CONTENTS

FOREWORD

As Wheaton's sixth president during its 125-year history, I am privileged to have predecessors who made indelible marks on the College through long and committed service.

Charles Albert Blanchard, second president, achieved the longest term in office—a remarkable forty-three years. Son of Wheaton's founder and first president, Jonathan Blanchard, Charles Albert learned the traits of perseverance, leadership, Christian integrity, and vision from his stalwart father.

Born in Galesburg, Illinois in 1848, where his father was then president of Knox College, Charles later attended Wheaton Academy and graduated from Wheaton College in 1870. He became principal of the Academy in 1872, professor at the College in 1874, vice-president in 1878, and president in 1882. He was ordained by College Church in Wheaton, serving five years as its pastor. He later was a supply pastor at Moody Memorial Church in Chicago and assisted in fund-raising efforts to begin Moody Bible Institute.

He was a lecturer for the National Christian Association, conducting aggressive campaigns against secret societies, as did his father. He was first vice-president of the National Fundamentalist Association, a director of the Chicago Tract Society and the Africa Inland Mission, and vice-president of the Christian and Missionary Alliance.

As president of Wheaton College, he was much in demand as a lecturer and writer and thereby extended the influence of the College and made known its uncompromising stand for the essential doctrines of the Christian faith. He continued actively in office until his death in 1925.

This book is his testimony that God answers prayer for those who put simple faith in Him. Blanchard expressed his motivation for writing it: "I know that God answers prayer, and I desire to help other people to know that He answers prayer." I became acquainted with this book during my first year as president at Wheaton College and found it both informative and challenging. I commend the volume to you, as appropriately reissued on this 125th anniversary of the College Charles Blanchard loved and served.

J. Richard Chase
Sixth President
Wheaton College
January 1985

INTRODUCTORY

Man is incurably religious.
Man is incurably prayerful.

I suppose every thoughtful person from time to time takes up with himself the question of prayer. How can God answer prayer if He be all-knowing and all-powerful? Why should One who could create a universe like this care to listen to beings like us, so ignorant, so short-lived, so sinful, so helpless?

Nevertheless, the impulse to prayer is irresistible. I was talking with a lad not long since, and asked him if he prayed. He replied, "Yes, sometimes."

I asked, "When do you pray?"

He answered, "When I get scared." He was not peculiar in this respect; in a cyclone or in a storm at sea, in a time of deathly illness or of financial disaster, men pray. They do not have to be taught; they simply pray. Even those who call themselves atheists reach out into the dark for God.

Does It Really Do Any Good?

Men pray without regard to this question; but after the storm and stress have passed, the question recurs. Even Christians who pray habitually and constantly from time to time have this question suggested to them.

My little boy, eleven years of age, tells his mother that it does no good to pray. He says, "I ask God to make me a good boy and He does not do it." He already has the prayer problem in its essence fully developed in his mind. Ministers have the same experience that my boy has. They tell

7

us plainly that their prayers are unanswered. Parents tell us the same thing. They say they pray for their children and that their prayers are not answered. Men and women in business life say the same. All intelligent people from time to time ask, "Does it do any good? If it does, what good does it do?"

Of Making Books, There Is No End

There are many books on prayer. Why should one add to the number? Many of these books are excellent. One of the most remarkable of them is *The Prayer Life* by Andrew Murray. He has been my great teacher in respect to prayer. I heard him many years ago at Northfield say repeatedly to D.L. Moody, "Mr. Moody, there must be more prayer. The speaking here is excellent, but there is too much of it in proportion to prayer."

We do not have time to pray. We get tired when going to meetings, listening to men. We must have more time to speak to God and to listen to Him. This subject burned in Mr. Murray's very bones, the crying, absolute necessity of prayer, if Christians were to live victorious lives.

Another book on this subject is by Dr. W.E. Biederwolf. It is entitled, *How Can God Answer Prayer?* A work smaller than either of these is *Preacher and Prayer* or *Power Through Prayer*, written by a brother with whom I have had no acquaintance, Rev. E.M. Bounds of Washington, Georgia. In conferences I have attended, this book is one of the most useful and popular among the students. The first book on prayer which I ever read, *The Silent Hour*, by Professor Austin Phelps, was a classic when I was in college and is still one of the best treatises on the subject.

The most powerful series of addresses I ever heard on the subject was by Dr. R.A. Torrey on "The Prayer Life of Jesus." Sermon after sermon was an examination of the method of prayer followed by our Lord. The series was conscience-quickening, faith-provoking, and inspiring.

Why, Then, Another Book?

For many reasons. In the first place, there are a great many people in the world who need to pray, and who suffer

8

because they do not know how. Many tens of thousands have never read the books I have mentioned, or any others on this subject. Another book may possibly appeal to a different set of persons.

Still further, the fact that a number of people have uttered their testimony is no reason why still others should not do the same. Every man is responsible for his own message. Every man has his own friends and acquaintances, and all men who know that God answers prayer have a duty to those who do not know. The performance of this duty is an imperative. Men are not conscience-free unless they perform it.

I have been wonderfully helped by the writers named. This makes me a debtor and I am ready to pay the debt as God makes it possible, for *I know that God answers prayer.* I desire to help other people to know that He answers prayer, so that sick ones, tempted ones, burdened ones, perplexed ones, weary ones, may find the wisdom and help, and comfort and strength which have come to me through prayer.

If an excuse is required for another book on this all-important subject, I think it is found in what I have written above. It is my earnest desire that this book should be of service. I have no desire to write a learned book. I have no desire to write a large book. My wish is that God shall help me write a book for real service to His people and I hope to put it in a form where the busy and the burdened may be able to derive benefit from it.

Charles A. Blanchard
Wheaton, Illinois
1915

PART ONE

WHAT IS IT TO PRAY?

Our four theological professors, with more than two hundred ministers, missionaries, and theological students came together with the [sin of prayerlessness] as the keynote of our meeting. From the very first in the address, there was the tone of confession, as the only way to repentance and restoration. At a subsequent meeting the opportunity was given for testimony as to what might be the sins which made the life of the church so feeble. Some began to mention failings that they had seen in other ministers, either in conduct, or in doctrine, or in service. It was soon felt that this was not the right way; each must acknowledge that in which he himself was guilty.

The Lord graciously so ordered it that we were gradually led to the sin of prayerlessness as one of the deepest roots of the evil. No one could plead himself free from this. Nothing so reveals the defective spiritual life in minister and congregation as the lack of believing and unceasing prayer. Prayer is in very deed the pulse of the spiritual life. It is the great means of bringing to minister and people the blessing and power of heaven. Persevering and believing prayer means a strong and an abundant life.

Andrew Murray

CHAPTER ONE

TALKING WITH GOD

It is safe to say that there is no subject on which persons think so carelessly as on the subject of religious faith and duty. Yet no subject is so important for time and for eternity. Our religious lives determine our social, political, industrial, commercial, and educational careers. There is nothing about which we ought to think so exactly and carefully as the subject of personal religion. It is safe to say, however, that there is no topic on which the average man or woman thinks more loosely, negligently, or inexactly, than this one.

Jesus told men to search the Scriptures (John 5:39). We all know what searching is. We have searched rooms, barns, bureau drawers, desks for valuable papers, agricultural implements, articles of clothing, books. We know how to *search*, but comparatively few of us search the *Scriptures*.

Some say they have not time. Some give other excuses and reasons for this neglect. When men do not search the Scriptures, they do not do other things which they ought to do. How can they even know what God requires unless they search the Scriptures? How can they pray unless they search the Scriptures? The result of carelessness in regard to this matter is deplorable ignorance on the part of multitudes, even of professed Christians, as to what prayer really is.

I always shrink when I hear the phrase "unanswered

prayer," for I question whether there is or can be such a thing. It is undoubtedly true that multitudes of people do what they call praying and do not derive benefit therefrom. But are the things which go by this name always prayer?

"Lord, Teach Us To Pray"

This was the petition of disciples who came to Jesus, desiring that He would aid them in this matter. He did not refuse the help they asked. He told them how to pray and He told them what great things even a small bit of faith would accomplish, if they really prayed. "When you pray, say, 'Our Father.'" "If you have faith like a grain of mustard seed, you can overturn mountains or pluck up trees by the roots." This is the teaching of our Lord. It is obvious that the force which is to accomplish such results is not a trifling power, but a power that can shake and destroy and build up.

Let us therefore seek to know what it is to pray. Let us come as the disciples did, asking the Lord to teach us to pray. And that He may teach us to pray, let us ask Him to teach us what prayer is.

Not a Form of Words

It is clear that prayer is not simply repeating words. Prayer utters itself in words orally, or otherwise, but uttering words is not necessarily prayer. The Pharisee stood and prayed thus *with himself.* The publican would not lift up his eyes to heaven, but stood afar off, and said, "God be merciful to me a sinner" (Luke 18:13). The Pharisee did not pray. He made a speech to God, a very poor speech too, by the way, one which has come down through the ages as a sort of monstrosity.

The publican did pray and he received an answer to his prayer. He went down to his house justified. Even if the Pharisee had used the words of the publican, he would not really have prayed if he had not had the spirit of the publican. God looks upon the hearts of men. He cannot be deceived and He will not be mocked. If we repeat words to Him which do not correspond to our heart attitude, He considers it an insult and an offense. He does not answer such pretended prayers except by judgments.

What Is the Prayer Attitude?

It is unquestionably a childlike state of mind and heart. "When you pray, say, 'Our Father.' " If I say, "My father," to a man who does not occupy that relation to me, it is simply a sort of lie. I must then, when I begin to pray, occupy the child position. What is the heart attitude of a child?

In the first place, perhaps, the attitude of loving confidence. God has given me nine children. Two of them are with the Lord, lovely children they were. When my children who remain say, "My father," they have a perfect confidence that if what they desire is within my power and judged to be helpful to them, they will get the thing which they desire. They had this confidence fully developed when they were just beginning to talk. It has not grown less as days have gone on. They have said, "My father," and they have felt, "My father," when they said it.

● Submission and Obedience. A child who is not submissive and obedient is not in any real sense a spiritual child, but rather a spiritual rebel. It is not difficult for one to know whether he is disposed to a loving submission and a constant obedience. This is simply a question of fact and anyone who will take the time to think it over will know whether he is at heart a child or a rebel. If he is really a rebel, it avails nothing for him to be talking as if he were a child. God is not pleased with what he says because He knows what he means. It is an offense, not a compliment, not a satisfaction, to say; "My Father," when in fact he has not the heart of a child.

● Self-Examination. It is possible that in years gone by, there was too much time spent in what was called "self-examination." Persons became morbid. They dwelt on their own states and attitudes so much that they lost the sense of God. It is very doubtful whether this is a common feeling at the present time. Personally, I am sure that a larger measure of self-examination would have been very helpful to me.

I remember my dear brother, Henry L. Kellogg, one of

the purest, sweetest, truest men I ever knew, a man to whom under God, I owe my own salvation. It was his custom when we were in college to have regular seasons for examining himself. I think this was one secret of his spiritual power and of his large usefulness. I believe that no man can say, "My Father," to God intelligently and acceptably, who does not from time to time raise with himself the question respecting the child attitude.

● Becoming as Little Children. "Except ye be converted, and become as little children, ye shall not enter into the kingdom of heaven" (Matt. 18:3). The little child trusts and the little child submits and the little child actively obeys, because he heartily loves his father. He comprehends very little of his father's plans. Almost all he knows is that his father occupies a certain position with regard to him, and his heart goes out to his father in a loving confidence that ever leads to larger measures of affection and service.

When we have prayed, or have done the thing which we have called praying, what has been our attitude of mind respecting God? Have we looked upon Him as a worthy child looks upon a worthy parent? Have we seriously thought of Him at all? Or have we, driven by some sense of need or some feeling of guilt, simply called because we must call? If so, then we have not prayed. No matter what we have named the thing which we have done, we may be sure that we have not prayed, for prayer is a heart attitude.

If an earthly parent should be approached by a child with a petition and should read the heart of the child and see that he did not love, that he did not trust, that he was not willing to obey, that he was really in a state of antagonism. He would at once feel that he could not be on fatherly relations until the child should come into the child attitude.

Let me repeat once more: It is entirely possible for every one who reads these words to know whether he is in the child state or not. If he is not, he cannot even *begin* to pray. He cannot say, "My Father," and all the time which he spends in pretended prayer while in this rebellious attitude is worse than thrown away. "When ye pray, say, 'Our Father.' " If you can truly say this, you are in a state to begin your prayer. If you cannot truly say this, you are not in a state to begin your prayer; so let us be sure in regard to this.

This is an article of cardinal importance. There is no progress, no beginning, without it. Only the child heart can acceptably say, "My Father," and if we have not the child heart, we are not children. We may belong to the church; we may occupy official positions in it; we may even be preachers of the Gospel, but the Lord will say to us in the great day, "I know you not whence ye are; depart from Me, all ye workers of iniquity" (Luke 13:27). "For let not that man think that he shall receive anything of the Lord" (James 1:7).

Prayer is the pulse of life; by it the doctor can tell what is the condition of the heart. The sin of prayerlessness is a proof for the ordinary Christian or minister, that the life of God in the soul is in deadly sickness and weakness.

Much is said, and many complaints are made about the feebleness of the church to fulfill her calling, to exercise an influence over her members, to deliver them from the power of the world, and to bring them to a life of holy consecration to God. Much is also spoken about her indifference to the millions of heathen whom Christ entrusted to her, that she might make known to them His love and salvation. What is the reason why many thousands of Christian workers in the world have not a greater influence? Nothing save this—the prayerlessness of their service. In the midst of all their zeal in the study and in the work of the church, of all their faithfulness in preaching and conversation with the people, they lack that ceaseless prayer which has attached to it the sure promise of the Spirit and the power from on high. It is nothing but the sin of prayerlessness which is the cause of the lack of a powerful spiritual life! *Andrew Murray*

CHAPTER TWO

WHAT IS AN
ANSWER TO PRAYER?

I have repeatedly heard beloved brethren say that when God declined to do the things which His children desired, the answer was as real as when He granted the thing which they desired. The statement is often made in this manner: "God says sometimes yes and sometimes no. No is as much an answer as yes, so that prayer is always answered."

It has ever seemed to me a cruel trifling with the souls of men to teach this. Of course, I do not mean to charge those who thus speak with intentional cruelty or trifling. Nevertheless, what they do seems to me a heartbreaking piece of work.

Here, for example, is a mother praying for the life of a child. As well as she knows how, she asks God to spare the life of her child, but she does not know exactly what prayer is. She has never been taught how to pray. In some essential particulars, her requests do not take the form of acceptable prayer.

God cannot grant her the thing that she desires in consistence with His own character. Her child dies. She is perplexed and distressed. She says to her religious advisor, "God has refused my prayer." He says, "Oh no, God has not refused your prayer. He has just said no."

I do not believe that this teaching is true, and I am sure it would not be a comfort to a mother whose heart lies cold and heavy under the shadow of the little grave.

When Business Troubles Harass

Here is a man who is in business difficulty. According to his best light, he prays for relief from his financial embarrassments, but he does not know much about prayer. He has not been a praying man. He has been a man of the world, though a member of the church. He has not been a student of the Bible and does not know what it teaches on the subject of prayer or what the conditions of acceptable prayer are. Blindly, ignorantly, he thinks he prays to God for relief. It does not come and his bank note goes to protest. His estate is scattered to creditors and he becomes bankrupt. He says, "Why did not God answer my prayer?" The fact may be that he never prayed at all. But his religious advisor says to him, "God has answered your prayer, but He answered no." I do not believe that teaching of this kind would be helpful to the afflicted person. He could justly look upon this explanation as trifling with his serious difficulty.

When the Tempter Assails

Here is a man who is in sore temptation. The world and the flesh and Satan conspire to destroy him. Opportunity coincides with inclination and he falls into shameful sin. His name is dishonored. His family is broken up. The church of Christ suffers. The neighborhood in which he lives is demoralized by his sin. At the time when temptation was strong upon his soul, he asked God to deliver him. He thinks he prayed and he says that his prayer was unanswered. He believes that it is possible for men to pray and not to recieve the thing that they desire. He goes to his religious advisor, who says to him, "Oh yes, Brother, your prayer was answered. God just said no."

I think such teaching would tend to make infidels rather than Christians, for this man very likely was like the one of whom I spoke a moment ago, a man who had never prayed in his life, a man who had never had the child spirit. He did not love God but he loved *things*, loved to eat, loved to drink, loved to wear good clothes, loved to live in a good house, and he gave his heart and mind to things. He read the newspapers and magazines, anything except the Bible, never searched the Scriptures, never knew what God required of men who prayed. He did not really know how to pray but cried out in the time of stress as a wild animal groans when caught in a cyclone, or when it feels the pull of the halter that is drawing it up to the killing block. Why should such a person say that God has not answered his prayer? Why should he be told that God has answered his prayer but has said no? The fact is, the poor man has not prayed.

I do not forget that God is very patient with our ignorances and that where He finds the heart right He attaches small importance to words. But He does attach importance to heart attitude. If the heart does not pray, the man does not pray, no matter what his words may be. We ought not to say to persons who do not pray, have not prayed, do not know how to pray, that God answers their prayers no instead of yes.

When God Answers Prayer

An answer to prayer is a granting of the thing which a child asks of his heavenly Father, according to the directions which his Father has clearly set down. If a saint prays for healing for himself or his child or his friend, and God answers his prayer, the sick person will recover. If a saint prays in scriptural fashion for relief from financial difficulties, he will be relieved. If he prays in scriptural fashion for victory over the the powers of evil, he will obtain victory. An answer to prayer is a granting of the thing desired. Saying no to a request is not an answer to prayer in any real, substantial meaning of the expression. When God answers prayer, He says yes.

If men have made many petitions which they consider prayers which have not been realized, the first question to ask is whether or not they have really prayed. Of course, it would be of help to them to decide first whether or not God always does answer prayer. If He does not, if it is true that saying no is an answer to prayer in the sense in which ordinary people use the term, then he need not be surprised. If at times God does not answer, all the sufferer can do is to submit to the inevitable.

But if an answer to prayer means the granting of the thing for which request is made, then God answers prayer or He does not. If God does not answer and, if there is a difficulty with himself—if his prayer is not prayer but a form, a pretense—then there may be help. If he can learn the difficulty and remove it, he may receive the answer which he desires.

I believe the question discussed in this chapter to be of the first importance. If this teaching is correct, then the one who has brought his request and has not received his answer is put upon an investigation. If answered prayer is not prayer which produces the result desired, then another course is obviously called for. Whatever may be found to be true as to this question will determine the whole prayer life of the Christian.

In an elders' prayer meeting, a brother put the question: "What, then, is the cause of so much prayerlessness? Is it not unbelief?"

The answer was: "Certainly; but then comes the question—What is the cause of that unbelief?" When the disciples asked the Lord Jesus: "Why could not we cast the devil out?" His answer was: "Because of your unbelief." He went further, and said: "Howbeit this kind goeth not out but by prayer and fasting." If the life is not one of self-denial—of fasting, that is, letting the world go; of prayer, that is, laying hold of heaven—faith cannot be exercised. A life lived according to the flesh and not according to the Spirit—it is in this that we find the origin of the prayerlessness of which we complain. As we came out of the meeting a brother said to me, "That is the whole difficulty; we wish to pray in the Spirit, and at the same time walk after the flesh, and this is impossible."

If one is sick and desires healing, it is of prime importance that the true cause of the sickness be discovered. This is always the first step towards recovery. If the particular cause is not recognized, and attention is directed to subordinate causes, or supposed but not real causes, healing is out of the question. In like manner, it is of the utmost importance for us to obtain a correct insight into the cause of the sad condition of deadness and failure in prayer in the inner chamber, which should be such a blessed place for us. Let us seek to realize fully what is the root of this evil.

Andrew Murray

CHAPTER THREE

CAN A SINNER PRAY?

When you pray, say, "My Father." Of course, the person who honestly and sincerely says, "My Father, " is not an unrepentant, unpardoned sinner. The one who can truly say, "My Father," has passed from death into life. There is one petition an unsaved soul can really offer to God, the petition for salvation. When it is honestly offered, the soul passes from death into life.

A child can ask his father for anything in the wide world, provided he maintains his child heart. A rebel can sincerely ask for only one thing—he can ask for pardon. When he has been pardoned, he has ceased to be a rebel and has become a good citizen in the kingdom of God. Then he has the rights of the citizens in that kingdom and can pray for the things he desires, provided he maintains the attitude of a good citizen.

If he should drop into a nonsubmissive state, he reassumes the character of a rebel. If he drops into the attitude of an unbelieving soul, while in that statea, he cannot say, "My Father" in his heart. Of course, he can say it with his mouth. If he does, he simply insults God; but having become a child of God, in answer to the prayer for pardon, he still has the right of access and he can pray.

Suppose that I am a backslider and I am not sorry for my backsliding. I am sorry because I am sick or because I need money or because my child disgraces me. Or I am sorry because I have not a paying position or because I am likely to lose a paying position. Without repentance for my backsliding, without confession or promise of amendment, I come to the place of prayer and ask God for healing, for money, for the salvation of my child so that he may not disgrace me anymore, or any one of ten thousand things. Being yet a rebel, how can I come into court? My hands are not clean, my heart is not right. I simply cannot say, "My Father," in my heart. I am not as a child of God in my heart attitude, and my prayer is an abomination to God. "If I regard iniquity in my heart, the Lord will not hear me" (Ps. 66:18). I have not the child heart. If I *say*, "My Father," but do not *think* or *feel*, "My Father," I do not even *will* that God should be my Father. I need help.

What, then, should this sinner do? He should cease to be a sinner. He should pass into the child attitude. When he occupies this position he can pray. To undertake prayer while in the state of an alien, a rebel, and an apostate, is to seek to mingle oil and water. They do not go together. If God should listen to sinners—I mean unrepentant sinners, rebellious sinners, sinners who say, "My Father," with their mouths while they say, "Myself," "My family," "My business," with their minds—He would be offering a premium on hypocrisy. This He certainly does not do, will not do, ought not to do. But when the sinner feels his sin, is sorry for his sin, is ready to cease from his sin, then God is ready to hear, ready to forgive, ready to receive, ready to reinstate in the kingdom of Christ.

Sinners cannot pray for anything but pardon, honestly and sincerely. When they are pardoned, they can pray for what they will, provided they maintain the child attitude and ask according to the directions which God has given for children. Of course, they cannot, when they are children, ask as if they were rebels or aliens. They must ask like children. If they are really children, so far as God gives them light, they will so ask; and if they so ask, then they will receive the things which they desire of God.

The Christian who is still carnal has neither disposition nor strength to follow after God. He rests satisfied with the prayer of habit or custom; but the glory, the blessedness of secret prayer is a hidden thing to him, till some day his eyes are opened, and he begins to see that "the flesh," in its disposition to turn away from God, is the archenemy which makes powerful prayer impossible for him.

I had once at a conference spoken on the subject of prayer, and I made use of strong expressions about the enmity of "the flesh" as a cause of prayerlessness. After the address, the minister's wife said that she thought I had spoken too strongly. She also had to mourn over too little desire for prayer, but she knew her heart was sincerely set on seeking God. I showed her what the Word of God said about "the flesh," and that everything which prevents the reception of the Spirit is nothing else than a secret work of "the flesh." Adam was created to have fellowship with God, and enjoyed it before his fall. After the fall, however, there came immediately a deepseated aversion to God, and he fled from Him. This incurable aversion is the characteristic of the unregenerate nature, and the chief cause of our unwillingness to surrender ourselves to fellowship with God in prayer. The following day she told me that God had opened her eyes; she confessed that the enmity and unwillingness of "the flesh" was the hidden hindrance in her defective prayer life. *Andrew Murray*

CHAPTER FOUR

DO ALL CHRISTIANS PRAY?

J esus spoke a parable to His disciples to this end, "that men ought always to pray, and not to faint" (Luke 18:1). I heard Dr. Maclaren in his lecture room at Manchester, England give an address from the text: "I had fainted, unless I had believed to see the goodness of the Lord in the land of the living" (Ps. 27:13). It was an evening hour and the chapel was filled with people. A single gas jet was burning over his head. This furnished light enough to show him to the people and to enable him to read as he went on with his lecture.

When he came to the end of his address he said, "Brethren, you have fainted. You know that you have fainted and you will faint unless you believe to see the goodness of the Lord in the land of the living."

There are many times in the lives of Christians when they do not pray. James is clear on this point. His letter is addressed to the people of God. He says, "To the twelve tribes which are scattered abroad . . . My brethren, count it all joy when ye fall into divers temptations" (James 1:1-2). It is these people to whom he says: "Ye lust, and have not; ye kill, and desire to have, and cannot obtain; ye fight and war, yet ye have not, because ye ask not" (James 4:2).

One may ask, "How can a person be a Christian without prayer?" The answer is easy. He cannot be the Christian he ought to be. He cannot be the Christian God desires him to be, commands him to be. "But we have this treasure in

earthen vessels" (2 Cor. 4:7). "For in many things we offend all" (James 3:2). If we all lived according to our privileges, we should all live prayerfully. But we do not all live
according to our privileges and sometimes Christians do not
pray. James was writing to his brothers in the faith when he
said, "Ye have not, because ye ask not."

I am satisfied that there is no one thing which more
hinders Christians from obtaining the things which they
ought to desire, the things which in a way they do desire,
than that they do not ask. Why do not Christians really ask
in God's way, according to God's mind, that they may receive the things which they need? There are many reasons
for this.

They Do Not Think
It is the natural impulse of the human heart to struggle for
the good things it desires. This is a part of the human
constitution as received from God. Within limits, it is a
correct impulse, for God offers no premiums on laziness.
But human effort disassociated from the divine is a poor
thing, and right here is the difficulty with us when we do
not think to pray.

A sincere Christian never sets up a Declaration of Inde-
pendence from God. He knows that unless he has help
from above, all his efforts will be in vain. Yet it is one thing
to know this fact and a very different thing to keep it in
mind and practically apply it.

Oftentimes I clearly see needs, real needs, which I am
sure are according to the will of God to supply. Without
thought of prayer I have undertaken to supply those needs.
I have not undertaken to supply them in any illegitimate
way. I have simply attempted to accomplish what needed
to be done. After effort for a longer or shorter time, I have
awakened to the fact that I have not prayed; that is, that I
have not committed that particular thing definitely to God.
Sometimes it has been the need of money, sometimes the
need of victory over temptation, sometimes the salvation of
other persons, sometimes the growth of grace of Christian
friends, and I have found that I have not received because I
have not asked.

They Do Not Believe

Another reason why Christians do not pray as they ought is because they do not believe. That is, they do not believe that God will give them the things which they desire. They believe that God is good. They believe that He does very many good things, that He watches over people and cares for them; but they do not have faith for the particular thing which they desire. Perhaps they have not thought about it in relation to God. They may have not raised the question whether it is according to His will or may have taken this for granted. Or perhaps they have really in their minds doubted whether the thing which they desire is according to the mind of God. In one way or another, faith is hindered. There is no loving trust for the thing desired.

If you were to stop them when they were feeling their need and ask, "Do you believe that God will grant you this thing?" and they were to answer honestly, they would be compelled to say, "No."

I have been astonished at myself in this regard to see how many times I have labored long and earnestly to secure the accomplishment of results which I believed to be right, and which I still believe to have been right, but without any definite committal of the affairs in question to God.

They Are Too Busy

Another reason why Christians do not pray is that they are too busy about other things. Most Bible prayers are short; but it is obvious from the life stories of the holy men who prayed, that they were continually in a state of prayer. No one can doubt that Daniel in Babylon took some time to pray. It is recorded of our Lord that He continued in prayer all night, and Paul speaks of Epaphras "always laboring fervently for you in prayers" (Col. 4:12).

All these expressions indicate time. I will not say that in every case those who thus labored fervently and strove earnestly in prayer stood apart from other activities while they were engaged in prayer, but evidently their minds were fastened on God. They looked to Him as the source of the good things which they desired, so that they were in a prayerful state. No man, even if he be a Christian, should so lose himself in the business and pleasures of the world that he neglects to take time to pray. Time is the indispensable element in the case. The man who will not spend time simply cannot pray and he will not have the things which he needs, the things which he might have.

"I am driven from morning till night. I am a busy mother. I have four children and no hired girl. There are three meals to be prepared each day for six people. There is a washing to be done fifty-two times a year. There is ironing to be looked after. There are clothes to be mended and stockings to be darned. How can I take time to pray?" This is a hard case.

The mother is tied down by tasks which are actually crushing in their character. What can the mother do? It is certain that if she does not pray, she is likely to be in a condition where she cannot do the work which is crowding upon her. Sanitariums are ever enlarging their borders. Mental hospitals cannot keep pace with the increase of population. Women with frazzled nerves are about us on every side. They are not all of the working class, either. Some of them are the wealthy ones who spend their time in various social duties, as they call them, but who have little or no actual physical labor to perform for their homes; yet they are broken down. The reason is that they are not in touch with God. They believe that He is, they desire to belong to Him in a sort of way, but they do not have time to read the Bible. They do not have time to pray. They do not have time to go to the prayer meeting. Some of them have time to attend card parties. Some of them have time to give dances for their children. Some of them have time to witness exhibits which, when they were young and untainted by the world, would have startled and made them ashamed.

Some of them have time for dressmakers who clothe perishing bodies in garments which will not afford any particular satisfaction when looked at from eternity, but they do not have time to pray. They do not have time for the Bible. They do not have time for the assemblies of God's people.

But all of these busy people who have no time for God will, by and by, have time to be sick. Many of them will have time to seek for health over land and sea without discovering it. And, if the Lord tarry, all of them will take time to be coffined and buried. Who gives us time? Who knows how much we are to have? Has the One, who gives us all the time we are to enjoy, a claim on any portion of it? If we are not acquainted with Him, will we get on successfully in what we do undertake?

Ten thousand graves, ten thousand prisons, ten thousand hospitals for the insane, ten thousand sanitariums, all make the same answer, "We did not have time for God, so we had to take time for these."

Teach Your Children To Pray

It is a melancholy fact that when people do not have time for God, they frequently do not have time for their own flesh and blood. The fathers and mothers who have no time to pray, to study God's Word, to worship with God's people, seldom have time and disposition to train their children for God. When people do not take time to train their children for God, someone else will take time to train their children for other persons and places.

It is said that a little girl in a worldly home was permitted at one time to visit her grandfather. This was an old-fashioned Christian home, where each day there was time to pray, to read the Bible, to sing Christian hymns. After a few weeks her mother came to take her home. The child objected, for she wished to stay at her grandfather's. Her mother was mortified and somewhat nettled. She said to the child, "Do you not wish to go home with Mother?"

The child replied, "Yes, Mamma, I would like to go home with you, but you know there is not any God at our house. Grandpa has a God here at his house and I like to stay where there is a God."

Poor child! How perfectly she expressed the cry of the child heart. These words, I trust, will be read by many burdened, worried, tired fathers and mothers. Some of them are distressed because of their children. They cannot understand why their children do not do as they desire. Many of them can find the explanation in the language of the little girl. Have they not been reared in a home where, so far as external appearances are concerned, there is no God? And if they are reared in such a home, what do the parents expect?

There is no satisfaction for the human soul this side of the throne of God. Children feel this just as older people do. Children cannot lose themselves so readily in business and pleasure. If their parents will show them the way, they will gladly drink in the comforting truths which God has spoken for the help of His people. If the parents have time, they will rejoice to see the results of their labors. If they have no time, many of them will shed bitter tears over the results of their neglect.

Pray Always

Christians should pray about everything, about all their physical needs, their eyes, their teeth, their lungs, their hearts, rheumatism, headaches, everything.

They should pray for their children, for their bodies, for their minds, for their hearts. They should pray for them when they go to the city that they may be safeguarded from trains and cars. They should pray for them when they go to school, that they may be delivered from evil companions, that they may be helped in the performance of their work.

There is nothing for which Christians ought not to pray. They should pray about their occupations. They should pray about the management of their homes, about their financial needs, about uses of the money which God gives them. There is nothing which concerns a Christian that is a matter of indifference to God. If they do not pray, they will not have the things which they need, even though they are Christians. Few Christians pray for the many things God would gladly do for them. Jesus spoke to this end, "That men ought always to pray, and not to faint" (Luke 18:1).

"Praying always with all prayer and supplication in the Spirit" (Eph. 6:18). This should be the daily life of the Christian. When it is, the life is successful, beautiful, glorious. When it is not, the life is limited, crippled, confined, oftentimes filled with shame and terror. Therefore, brethren, let us pray always and about all things, and prove God if He is not still the One who hears and answers prayer.

What the church needs today is not more machinery or better, not new organizations or more and novel methods, but men whom the Holy Ghost can use—men of prayer, men mighty in prayer. The Holy Ghost does not flow through methods, but through men. He does not come on machinery, but on men. He does not anoint plans, but men—men of prayer.

The character as well as the fortunes of the Gospel is committed to the preacher. He makes or mars the message from God to man. The preacher is the golden pipe through which the divine oil flows. The pipe must not only be golden, but open and flawless, that the oil may have a full, unhindered, unwasted flow.

The real sermon is made in the closet. The man—God's man—is made in the closet. His life and his profoundest convictions were born in his secret communion with God. The burdened and tearful agony of his spirit, his weightiest and sweetest messages were got when alone with God. Prayer makes the man; prayer makes the preacher; prayer makes the pastor.

The pulpit of this day is weak in praying. The pride of learning is against the dependent humility of prayer. Prayer is with the pulpit too often only official—a performance for the routine of service. Prayer is not to the modern pulpit the mighty force it was in Paul's life or Paul's ministry. Every preacher who does not make prayer a mighty factor in hs own life and ministry is weak as a factor in God's work and is powerless to project God's cause in this world.

E.M. Bounds

CHAPTER FIVE

THE SIN
OF PRAYERLESSNESS

In Andrew Murray's book, *The Prayer Life,* he says that to live prayerlessly is a dishonor to God, that it is the cause of deficient spiritual life, that the church suffers dreadful losses as a result of prayerlessness in the ministry, and that it is impossible to preach the Gospel to all men unless this sin is overcome and cast out. He tells how a number of Christian ministers assembled in South Africa, burdened because of the needs of the church, and that in conference they concluded that the difficulties under which they labored were caused by the lack of prayer. There were four theological professors present, a number of theological students, and about two hundred ministers. As the meeting went forward, with one consent they admitted that prayerlessness was the source of the evils which grieved them. This led to an annual meeting which lasts for ten days and has produced great good in creating and maintaining spiritual life among the ministers and their congregations. (See the preceeding page.)

It is my impression that prayerlessness is very seldom thought of, confessed, and abandoned as a sin. To begin with, it is an omission, not a commission, and this class of wrongs is naturally looked upon as less offensive to God than actual transgressions of His commands.

Compare for a moment the two divine words, "Thou shalt not steal," and "Pray without ceasing." They are in the same revelation and both are in the imperative mode.

One is a negative and the other a positive. It is safe to say that the consciences of all people who read these words would instantly condemn them if they were to deliberately take property which did not belong to them. It is almost equally sure that very few of them would feel that their neglect of prayer was to be repented and confessed like a violation of the eighth commandment. Yet for a Christian to fail to pray without ceasing may do more injury to men than for someone to take what does not belong to him. We are so prone to read into the Word of God that which He has not put there.

He has never told us that certain commands are important and that others are not. When we reflect upon His character and our relation to Him, it is very dangerous to regard any of His commands as unimportant. Let us therefore think on this question until our minds are settled.

It Is Possible to Pray

First, let us remember that repeating prayer words is not praying, and that if we do this without sincere heart desire, we are insulting God—not honoring Him. Let us, in the second place, divest ourselves of the thought that what others do, or what we have been accustomed to doing, cannot be very sinful. There is a paralyzing power in evil habit, and there is also a paralyzing power in making men our standard instead of the Law of God.

Let us also remember that it is never impossible to do what God requires. I do not say that it is never difficult. I do not say that it is never costly in time, money, friends, ease. But I do say that it is never impossible. To hold and teach that God requires what man cannot do is irrationality and blasphemy. God is our Father and He adjusts all His requirements to our powers. Where the requirement is beyond our gifts, the gifts are increased. As someone has said, "The commands of God are always enablings."

It is possible for us to pray just as God requires us to. If we do not do this, we sin and the sin will stand against us until it is repented, confessed, and put away. We are, therefore, not dealing with a trifling matter, but with a question which affects our standing before God.

There is probably no one fact in modern life which has more seriously interfered with family prayer than the early and late trains which have become necessary in view of the complexity of modern life. When men worked in their homes, conditions were radically different. Men are now cogs in wheels and the wheel cannot turn if cogs are absent or broken. The result is that in every great city in the world, thousands of people, young, middle-aged and old, hasten from their homes in the morning and return to them late at night. How shall these persons share in the home prayer which used to characterize every Christian household? How shall they even have the time required for deliberate and effective personal prayer?

Along with this difficulty is the multiplicity of entertainments, meetings, social gatherings, and the like, which now draw so largely on the evening hours. When the day is crowded and the night is largely turned into day, how shall the soul quiet itself before God? How shall one obtain the time which is needful to successful prayer?

Along with this there is a mental difficulty. Doubts exist and add to the helplessness of prayer. Dr. Biederwolf's book, *How Can God Answer Prayer?* shows that it is possible that God should answer prayer. The very fact that such a book is written speaks volumes as to the mental condition of the Lord's people. A question like this would a few years ago have seemed as strange as it would be to ask if a hungry man will eat, or a duck will swim.

When I was a boy, almost everyone, even people who were not Christians at all, believed that God did answer prayer. I question whether even infidels would have asked whether or not He did so. Of course, an atheist would look on prayer to God as an absurdity, but no one who really believed in a Creator of the universe would question His power to grant a request if it were made.

More Than Spiritual Gymnastics

Men, who teach that God is in some way hampered by the regulations which He has made, so that it is difficult or impossible for Him to answer prayer, nevertheless hold that prayer may be useful. They teach that God does not give

36

the things which are asked for, but that the mere effort to approach Him is useful—that it puts men into a better state, that it awakens a sense of dependence and gratitude for favors received in the ordinary course of nature—in other words, that it is valuable to the person as an exercise, though it has no effect upon the action of God.

That prayer does have a helpful reaction on the human spirit is unquestionably true. But we are not so constituted that we take either spiritual, intellectual, or physical exercise regularly and through long periods of time without the expectation of some practical results. In other words, we wish to bring things to pass. We wish to see results. If we ask for favors, we hope to obtain them. If we ask for pardon or peace or purity or power or health or life or money or friends, or anything else from God, we hope to obtain it. And if we become satisfied that our prayers do not result in obtaining the things which we seek, we will cease praying.

The Sins of the False Teacher

If we have not erred thus far in this chapter, there are two or three things which are settled and one at least which will follow. Since God has commanded us to pray, we ought to pray and if we do not, we sin. If we commit this sin, we should repent, and confess, and reform. The fact that there are difficulties in the way is no excuse for neglecting to do this, for God knew all about the difficulties when He gave the commands, and He is quite able to furnish us strength to overcome them. If, therefore, men teach that God does not answer prayer, they sin against the souls of men. They not only commit the sin of prayerlessness themselves, but they teach men to commit this sin. They become centers of evil influences which go out in ever-widening circles. God alone can see the shores on which the dark waves break.

Each of us, therefore, should raise the questions: Am I a prayerless person? Do I teach other people to be prayerless? If I am a prayerless person, am I ready to admit that I am committing sin? And am I ready to cease from this sin—to ask pardon for it? As we reflect upon these weighty subjects, let us remember that if we know to do good and do not do it, we commit sin (James 4:17).

Brains and nerves may serve the place and feign the work of God's Spirit, and by these forces the letter may glow and sparkle like an illuminated text, but this glow and sparkle will be as barren of life as the field sown with pearls. The death-dealing element lies back of the words, back of the sermon, back of the occasion, back of the manner, back of the action.

The great hindrance is in the preacher himself. He has not in himself the mighty life-creating forces. There may be no discount on his orthodoxy, honesty, cleanness, or earnestness; but somehow the man, the inner man in its secret places, has never broken down and surrendered to God, his inner life is not a great highway for the transmission of God's message, God's power. Somehow self and not God rules in the holy of holies. Somewhere, all unconscious to himself, some spiritual nonconductor has touched his inner being, and the divine current has been arrested. His inner being has never felt its thorough spiritual bankruptcy, its utter powerlessness; he has never learned to cry out with an ineffable cry of self-despair and self-helplessness till God's power and God's fire come in and fill, purify, empower. Self-esteem, self-ability in some pernicious shape has defamed and violated the temple which should be held sacred for God.

Life-giving preaching costs the preacher much—death to self, crucifixion to the world, the travail of his own soul. Only crucified preaching can give life. Crucified preaching can come only from a crucified man. *E.M. Bounds*

CHAPTER SIX

DIALOGUE OR MONOLOGUE?

I am sure that prayer is answered and that we obtain a thousand good gifts from God because we ask for them. Yet apart from any individual result of prayer, there is a general blessing which is not likely to be overestimated and which we are in danger of neglecting. I speak of the opportunity of conversation with the Maker of the universe.

I heard Andrew Murray say that too many times we make prayer a monologue when it ought to be a dialogue. "Often we keep talking to God, asking for things, telling Him things, when He would like to have us stop and give Him an opportunity to speak to us. Many times it would be well if, in prayer, we should stop and say 'Father, what hast Thou to say to Thy child?' "

I was impressed with the same thought in an address I heard George Müller of Bristol, England give on the subject of securing texts. He said that ministers ought to be told what to preach about, just as any messenger would be given his commission by the one who sent him. He went on to say that he had for years been accustomed, when he did not know what to preach about, to ask from God and to receive his subject from Him. Mr. Müller spoke of talking with God exactly as we speak of talking with one another. I have no doubt that the conversation was just as real in his case as in the case of two men who speak with one another in the house or by the way.

Conversing with God

If we were permitted a familiar conversation with men and women distinguished by reason of excellence of character or of great achievement, we should consider it an honor and a privilege. Suppose that Florence Nightingale should come to your town, or the poet Longfellow, or the missionary Paul, or the statesman Gladstone. Suppose you should be invited to meet one of them at a dinner or at a social gathering—to sit by and to ask them questions and to listen to their replies. It would be a thing long remembered and often rehearsed. You would tell your children and, if possible, your children's children how you had seen and spoken with such a distinguished person.

But in prayer we are not speaking to a good person merely, but to One who has never been stained by even the shadow of a sin, One who has not only great powers but all powers, who made the worlds and all that they contain. He is in a peculiar relation to us, for we have been created in His image. We can know and enjoy, suffer or decide, rembember or imagine as He can. In prayer we are permitted conversation with this marvelous Person. We are invited to freely tell Him of everything which concerns us. We are permitted to ask from Him everything which the Holy Spirit allows us to ask. We are invited, commanded, urged to be free with Him.

In all the record of His dealings with men, there is not one instance in which He found fault with men for coming too frequently, for asking too largely. On the other hand, He at times reproved men because they asked too little or because they did not persevere. The whole spirit of His direction is "Open thy mouth wide, and I will fill it" (Ps. 81:10). Is it not strange that we value so lightly so great a privilege? Is it not remarkable that men have to be urged, argued with, entreated to appropriate an opportunity of this kind?

Ofttimes entertainments are given, consisting of readings from the works of great writers or poets. Where the men are great and their reputations are widespread, people flock in thousands to listen and pay large sums of money for the privilege. In prayer we are permitted to speak in a friendly and intimate way with the One who made these great men; and He promises to tell us everything we need to know, to forgive us all our transgressions if we repent and believe, to give wisdom in every time of perplexity, to give strength for every labor which we are ever called upon to perform.

We have the testimony of thousands, if we choose to listen, that He performs more than all that He has promised. It is to this conversation we are invited when we are taught to pray.

Walking With God

One of the most delightful methods of holding a conversation is to make it a part of a friendly walk. Speaking of Enoch's translation to heaven, someone has said, "He walked with God habitually, and one day he walked with Him so far that God said to him, 'It is not worthwhile to go back. Come home with Me.' So he walked on and never returned to earth again." It is one of the privileges of prayer that, when we are not permitted time for deliberation and separation, we can thus have these conversations with God in the midst of daily tasks. We can pray as we walk to trains and as we return through the streets at night from our day of toil. We can lift our hearts to God before a conversation which is important or in the pauses of the conversation. We can pray without ceasing—that is to say, we can always be in the spirit of prayer and always find it easy to send our hearts upward when the opportunity occurs. Thus we can walk and talk with the Almighty.

Unless we were assured of this by God Himself, we could not believe it to be true; for we are so conscious of our weakness, of our ignorance and our sin, that we should not believe it possible that God could thus favor us, except that He has taken such pains to make it sure.

Let us quietly wait before Him and seek in some measure to take in this wonderful thought, to really understand as well as we can what it means to talk with God. Then having so done, let us more faithfully avail ourselves of this high honor and wonderful privilege.

PART TWO

CONDITIONS OF SUCCESSFUL PRAYER

Long, discursive, dry, and inane are the prayers in many pulpits. Without unction or heart, they fall like a killing frost on all the graces of worship. Death-dealing prayers they are. Every vestige of devotion has perished under their breath. The deader they are, the longer they grow. A plea for short praying, live praying, real heart praying, praying by the Holy Spirit—direct, specific, ardent, simple, unctuous in the pulpit—is in order. A school to teach preachers how to pray, as God counts praying, would be more beneficial to true piety, true worship, and true preaching than all theological schools.

Stop! Pause! Consider! Where are we? What are we doing? Preaching to kill? Praying to kill? Praying to God! The great God, the Maker of all worlds, the Judge of all men! What reverence! What simplicity! What sincerity! What truth in the inward parts is demanded! How real we must be! How hearty! Prayer to God is the noblest exercise, the loftiest effort of man, the most real thing! Shall we not discard forever accursed preaching that kills and prayer that kills, and do the real thing, the mightiest thing—prayerful praying, life-creating preaching, bring the mightiest force to bear on heaven and earth and draw on God's exhaustless and open treasury for the need and beggary of man?

E.M. Bounds

CHAPTER SEVEN

SUBMISSION
TO GOD'S WILL

O My Father, if this cup may not pass away from Me, except I drink it, Thy will be done" (Matt. 26:42).

We are commanded to search the Scriptures. To search is to carefully investigate for the purpose of ascertaining what is within. Another expression which is important in this connection is found in 1 Corinthians 2:13: "Comparing spiritual things with spiritual." Spiritual things are preeminently revealed in the Word of God. If we compare spiritual things with spiritual, we will necessarily compare Scripture with Scripture.

Some persons who know very little about the Bible are accustomed to say that it is like an old fiddle—you can play on it any tune you wish. By this they mean to say that the teaching of the Bible is not clear, that it is self-contradictory, that persons who desire to know the will of God cannot ascertain it decisively from this Word. However, people who read the Bible on narrow lines for the purpose of proving some little sectarian proposition, or justifying themselves in some course of action which they desire to pursue, will give occasion for this reproach.

In regard to prayer, it is essential, if one wishes to know how to pray, not to take an isolated text here and there, but to take all Scriptures touching on this subject, compare Scripture with Scripture, be willing to accept anything which is shown to be true, and in this way arrive at the method of victorious praying. There are no real contradictions. There is a great and blessed harmony and anyone may thus come to the very truth of God respecting this great means of joy and service.

In an earlier chapter I spoke of the child spirit as a spirit of obedience. I desire in this chapter to treat this important subject in a way that will be helpful to some believers in attaining to this grace, which is an essential condition of real prayer.

An Attitude of Prayer

Anyone who will reflect for even a moment will see that this spiritual attitude is the only rational one, the only one which is at all likely to be successful. How absurd it would be for those so ignorant, so sinful and helpless as we, to come to God with predeterminations, to say to Him in heart, even if not in words, "I desire this thing whether You see it to be best for me or not." I do not say that persons who pray with this spirit never receive the things for which they ask. At times they do. The Word of God says that God gave to His people their requests but sent leanness into their souls (Ps. 106:15). That is to say, He gratified them, but the very thing which He gave them worked leanness into their souls.

There is no word spoken in God's Book concerning prayer more true than this one: "We know not what we should pray for" (Rom. 8:26). How can we know? We do not comprehend our own natures even. We know nothing at all of the future with its tests and needs. We know very little of the past. We illy comprehend the present. How is it possible for us to know what we should ask for? The fact is, a thoughtful man would in advance see that his only safety would be to say as Jesus did: "Nevertheless not My will, but Thine, be done" (Luke 22:42).

I find that some persons have not read a little story which has been oftentimes helpful to me. A gentleman, walking by one of the beautiful hedgerows in England, saw a little lad on his knees and, pausing a moment, heard him repeating his letters, "A, B, C, D, E, F, G." The little fellow went clear through the alphabet and when he had completed he began again, "A, B, C, D," to the end, and so he continued until he had repeated the alphabet perhaps half a dozen times after which he said, "Amen," and arose. The gentleman was puzzled and said to the little fellow, "Why, my boy, what have you been doing?"

He replied, "I was praying, sir."

The gentleman said, "Praying? But you were only saying your letters over and again."

The lad answered, "Yes. I don't know what to ask for, nor how to ask, so I thought I would say the letters to God a good many times and ask Him to put them together the right way Himself."

"Out of the mouth of babes and sucklings hast Thou ordained strength" (Ps. 8:2). It is safe to say that that little fellow, kneeling by the hedgerow, knew more of the essence of prayer than many who have taken all the training of the divinity schools. For when we are willing to say the letters to God and let Him put them together the way it will be best for us to have them placed, He is attracted by the confidence we have, just as we are attracted to those who believe in us.

Satisfaction With God's Will

Years ago I was giving a course of three lectures on secret societies Monday evenings at the Moody Church in Chicago. I delivered the first and second, and on the third Monday evening went down to my train. I found that the time had been changed and that there was no train over that line until 10 o'clock at night. I asked the representative of the road in Wheaton, "Is there no freight on which I can get to the city?"

"No," he said, "no freight train tonight."

I asked, "Could I not go by Aurora and get a train on the Burlington, or by Elgin and get a train on the Milwaukee?"

After studying the timecards awhile he said, "No, there is nothing either way." Then, thinking, he said, "Perhaps, if you should go over to West Chicago, you might catch a fast freight that would take you in in time."

So I stepped on to a train that was at the station and rode to West Chicago. I went through the same series of inquiries there and received the same replies. I finally asked to the agent, "What will you charge me for an engine to take me into the city?"

He said, "We could not send you in on an engine, but I will send you in on a car for $50."

I have never been rich, and at that time I was particularly poor, but I knew that there would be a large audience waiting for me in Chicago. Although I was not paid for the service and I had no money to pay for the special train, I knew I must go. So I said to him, "If you will get the car ready, I will be obliged to you and we will go at once." In a few moments the engine with the passenger coach attached was at the door and in due time I was landed in Chicago.

While the engineer was bringing out the special, I made out an obligation to the Northwestern Railway for $50. The agent said to me, "Perhaps they will not charge as much as this, but I would not dare to promise the service for less." The next morning I went to the general offices of the Northwestern Railway to see if I could get a reduction, for I really did not know how to pay the sum for which I had obligated myself. The president was not in; but since I was also acquainted with Mr. Whitman, at that time general superintendent and a courteous gentleman, I went into his office. I stated the case to him and said that in view of the fact that I was rendering public service, for which I received no compensation, and in view of the further fact that though I ought to have known that the train time was changed, I did not, and I thought perhaps he would reduce the charge somewhat.

He looked across his desk at me and asked, "Well, Mr. Blanchard, what would satisfy you?"

I replied, "I shall be satisfied with whatever Mr. Whitman says."

He smiled and replied, "Well, I think we will not make any charge this time." Of course, I attribute the fact that his mind and heart were moved to this generous act through the providence of God, to the action of His Holy Spirit. But so far as my part of the transaction was concerned, I think that the confidence which I reposed in him, and the willingness which I expressed to be satisfied with whatever he should say, was the ground of his generous deed.

The fact is, God has a right to lay out our lives. He has made plans for them and unless we resist, He will help us to live out those plans. When we pray we must say, either in words or in heart, "Nevertheless, not as I will, but as Thou wilt" (Matt. 26:39). A stubborn desire to have our own way about *anything* is entirely inconsistent with the act of prayer. When we thus come to God, no matter what we imagine ourselves to be doing, no matter what particular form of words we use, we are not really praying. God does not recognize our act as a prayerful act. He is offended. He may grant us the things that we desire. At times He does, but always there is a penalty, for it is not possible that we should thus come to God without purchasing evil for our own lives.

Willing To Be Made Willing

I have spoken of a number of my prayer teachers, men of God, who have done me good, have helped me much. There is another one whose name I am glad to record here as having been helpful to me in this regard. I speak of F.B. Meyer of London, known wherever the English language is spoken by his wonderful devotional books. I remember that he was teaching in our seminary in Chicago at one time, in a simple, straightforward way giving an account of his own experience. He said that at one time in his life he was conscious of the fact that he was not willing to live according to the plan of God. He tried, as men do, to make himself willing but failed. Still he found the rebellious spirit within and at last, in almost hopelessness, he said, "Lord, I am not willing, but I am willing to be made willing and You can make me willing. Please make me willing to do Your will."

Dr. Meyer's testimony was that when this was the prevailing prayer, almost immediately he found the hardness of heart wearing away, the stubborn will yielding, the unwillingness passing into a cheerful submission to the plan of God. Are you willing to be made willing to do the will of God? If you cannot honestly now from your heart say, "Nevertheless not my will, but Thine, be done," are you willing that God should enable you to thus pray? Do you desire that He should? Will you ask Him so to do? If you do, in sincerity, then for His own glory, for your good and for the help of those whom you may help, He will make you willing. If by nature your heart is as stubborn and unyielding as a mule's, He will make it like the heart of a little child, so that you will be enabled honestly to say, "My Father," and also to say from time to time, as occasion requires, "Nevertheless not my will, but Thine be done."

The little estimate we put on prayer is evident from the little time we give to it. The time given to prayer by the average preacher scarcely counts in the sum of the daily aggregate. Not infrequently the preacher's only praying is by his bedside in his nightdress, ready for bed and soon in it, with, perchance, the addition of a few hasty snatches of prayer ere he is dressed in the morning. How feeble, vain, and little is such praying compared with the time and energy devoted to praying by holy men in and out of the Bible? How poor and mean our petty, childish praying is beside the habits of the true men of God in all ages! To men who think praying their main business and devote time to it according to this high estimate of its importance does God commit the keys of His kingdom, and by them does He work His spiritual wonders in this world. Great praying is the sign and seal of God's great leaders and the earnest of the conquering forces with which God will crown their labors.

The preacher is commissioned to pray as well as to preach. His mission is incomplete if he does not do both well. The preacher may speak with all the eloquence of men and of angels; but unless he can pray with a faith which draws all heaven to his aid, his preaching will be "as sounding brass or a tinkling cymbal" for permanent God-honoring, soul-saving uses. *E.M. Bounds*

CHAPTER EIGHT

THANKSGIVING

Be careful for nothing, but in everything by prayer and supplication with thanksgiving let your requests be made known unto God. And the peace of God, which passeth all understanding, shall keep your hearts and minds through Christ Jesus" (Phil. 4:6-7).

I do not believe there is any sin more offensive to God, or more common among men, than the sin of ingratitude. We do not like it ourselves when we benefit persons, even in a trifling way, if we see clearly that they have no thanksgiving in their hearts. We are not pleased. It is not that we care for their thanks, nor that we would be encouraged by their gratitude. Rather, there is a feeling of injustice, a sense of meanness that comes over us when we see those whom we have helped give no thought to our efforts to do them good.

God is like us in this respect; He has perhaps the same feeling in greater measure, for He is the author not of some good, but of all good; not of trifling benefits, but of life and health and home and friends and a Saviour and salvation and keeping—the author of all good gifts. "Every good gift and every perfect gift is from above, and cometh down from the Father of lights, with whom is no variableness, neither shadow of turning" (James 1:17).

And He says that we are to make our requests with thanksgiving. I believe I have heard a thousand prayers for forgiveness to one prayer thanking God for forgiveness. When Jesus cleansed the ten lepers, one turned back to give thanks while nine went on their way. I have many times wondered whether those nine healed lepers came back into leprosy—whether they were healed at all. I am certain that if they were, Jesus who said with such a sorrowful tone, "Where are the nine?" was not pleased with them. How could He have been?

Keeping Confidences

A friend once said to me, "I do not like to speak about my relations to God and I do not like to hear other people talk about theirs. It seems to me like the confidences between lovers, which are not intended for the public ear, but belong to themselves." Of course, there are many things for which we pray that it would not be wise to mention in public assemblies, but even these might be mentioned in a general way; that is, if I do not wish to thank God in a public assembly for a definite answer to prayer, it is perfectly easy for me to say that I have received an answer and that I am grateful. Thus I give thanks in the congregation and at the same time I preserve the confidence of which my friend was speaking.

I once heard a burdened woman in the far west of Kansas praying. She asked for a number of things. Her heart was very heavily laden and then it was that she said, "As for things which are between me and Thee, I leave them before Thy throne." Her words seemed very beautiful to me then and they do now.

There are certain church prayer meetings where the voice of praise is continually heard. Such prayer gatherings are unspeakably delightful—to hear one thanking God for the salvation of a father, and another for the salvation of a husband, and a third for the salvation of a child, and a fourth for the healing of a sick one, and a fifth for the supplying of a need, and a sixth for the opening of a door to employment, and a seventh for the safe return of a friend and so on. Such a meeting is so different from one where the pastor gives a short sermon, then says to the people, "You are at liberty to use the time," and no one responds, all acting as though God had not done anything to make them glad or when they do pray, their prayers are sombre tones as though life were a burden, as if God were dead or dying. I do not believe that there is anything which could be done in our prayer meetings and church assemblies to quicken the fires of divine life in the souls of men more than to have an epidemic of thanksgiving.

Meeting the Condition

Thanksgiving is a condition of answered prayer. At times persons say to me, "Does not God know when I am thankful?" And I reply, "Certainly. He does and He is glad; but is that any reason why you should not do what He has bid you do?"

Between husbands and wives, parents and children, this same spirit of thanksgiving would work wonderful changes if it were given free play. There are many wives who seem to care little about husbands, except that they pay the bills. They are glad to live in homes which are furnished and provided; yet if they make any remark about it at all, it is generally to speak of some lack, something more which the husband might do.

I sat in a home not a great while ago and heard a wife, who had spent every dollar her husband could earn for years, some of it in wise and some in foolish ways, make a suggestion of this kind. Her husband was a gentleman and made no reply, but I watched his look and I am sure that if his wife had struck him across the face with a rawhide, he would not have flinched more in his soul than he did.

I read years ago of a mother who had raised six boys to manhood and, her work done, had lain down to die. The boys came home to see their mother, and her oldest son, a great, powerful man, knelt by her and, wiping the deathdew from her forehead, said to her, "Mother, you have always been a good mother to us boys."

The tired woman closed her eyes and great tears pushed out under the lids and ran down her wasted cheeks. Then she opened her eyes, looked searchingly into the face of her son, and asked, "My boy, is that really true? Do you boys feel that way about me?"

He replied, "Indeed we do, Mother. We often speak of what a good mother you have been to us."

Again she closed her eyes, and again great tears ran down her wasted cheeks, and then she opened her eyes and looked into the face of her firstborn and said to him, "My boy, I prayed more that I might be a good mother to you six boys than for anything else. I was afraid that I should fail in some way to be all that I ought to you, and I never knew whether you boys thought I had failed or not until now. Not one of you ever told me I was a good mother until today."

Was it not a tragedy that the dear mother should bear six sons, should nurse them through the sicknesses of babyhood, should make their clothes and wash them and iron them, should prepare their meals a thousand times a year until they were grown to manhood, should see them, one by one, move out into the world, all the while wondering in her heart if they thought she had been a success as a mother, and not one of the six should ever say, "You have been a good mother," until she was ready to die? They were good boys, good men, but they did not express their thanksgivings.

I am sure that there are good fathers and mothers by tens of thousands who are waiting as anxiously to hear a thankful word from a son or a daughter as that mother did, and I am sure that there are children who are waiting for the commendation of a father or a mother and who will be saved from ruin if they get it, and will perhaps lose their souls if they do not get it. How pitiful it is to hear parents or teachers always condemning, criticizing, speaking in harsh, strident tones, never saying, "Well done, well done." It is the death stroke to souls that might be happy, to lives that might be filled with service.

"With thanksgiving." That is the way to make requests. I am sure that at times it would be well if we should ask nothing of God at all, but simply rehearse to Him His mercies, so tireless, so faithful.

Counting Many Blessings

I was talking with a dear old saint recently who was on her deathbed. She was ninety-five years of age and had had what the world calls "a hard life." But she said to me, "Mr.

Blanchard, I set out the other day to count up the goodnesses of God. I do not know how long I counted, but I think I counted an hour, and then I found that I had not made a beginning. Why, I believe that if I should take a whole week, I could not simply name the goodnesses of God to me." I am certain that when she crossed into the country where the inhabitants do not say, "I am sick," the praises of that region were native to her. She did not need to learn them. She was accustomed to them as we all ought to become accustomed to them.

Can ambition, that lusts after praise and place, preach the Gospel of Him who made Himself of no reputation and took on Him the form of a servant? Can the proud, the vain, the egotistical preach the Gospel of Him who was meek and lowly? Can the bad-tempered, passionate, selfish, hard, worldly man preach the system which teems with long-suffering, self-denial, tenderness, which imperatively demands separation from and crucifixion to the world? Can the hireling official, heartless, perfunctory, preach the Gospel which demands the Shepherd to give His life for the sheep? Can the covetous man, who counts salary and money, preach the Gospel till he has cleansed his heart and can say in the spirit of Christ and Paul in the words of Wesley: "I count it dung and dross; I trample it under my feet; I (yet not I, but the grace of God in me) esteem it just as the mire of the street, I desire it not, I seek it not"? God's revelation does not need the light of human genius, the polish and strength of human culture, the brilliancy of human thought, the force of human brains to adorn or enforce it; but it does demand the simplicity, the docility, humility, and faith of a child's heart.

E.M. Bounds

CHAPTER NINE

CONFESSION
AND INTERCESSION

I take the subject of this chapter from the directions which the Holy Spirit gives through James for the care of the sick: "Is any sick among you? Let him call for the elders of the church; and let them pray over him, anointing him with oil in the name of the Lord. And the prayer of faith shall save the sick, and the Lord shall raise him up; and if he have committed sins, they shall be forgiven him. Confess your faults one to another, and pray one for another, that ye may be healed. The effectual fervent prayer of a righteous man availeth much" (James 5:14-16).

Francis Murphy used to say, "The three hardest words to pronounce in the English language are, 'I was wrong,' and the next three hardest to pronounce are, 'You were right.' " Honest confession of faults is one of the most difficult things that Christians ever have to do.

Satan knows that if we honestly confess our sins, they are forgiven. He knows that if we honestly confess them we cease from them. Therefore he fights every inch of the road that a Christian walks toward confession.

A Personal Incident

I remember some years ago when Mrs. Blanchard was quite sick. She is a physician and has been, by the grace of God, a very successful one. I have myself seen her, under God, raise a young man from the very edge of the grave, when the physician in charge was letting him die as fast as he could. I have never been particularly disturbed when she has been ill, thinking that she knew what to do, would do it, and that shortly she would be well. At the time of which I am speaking, she took the remedies which she had given to many others, but for some reason they produced no satisfactory results. Days grew into weeks, and weeks into months, and there was no improvement. She began to look really haggard and sick. She said to me one day, "I do not believe I shall be any better unless I go to the hospital and have an operation. If you will call up the Presbyterian Hospital and arrange for a room, I will see Dr. Sarah Hackett Stevenson and ask her if she will operate on me." I called the hospital and arranged for the room. She saw Dr. Stevenson, who agreed to operate.

We were waiting a day or two, when she said to me, "I think perhaps I would like to go down to Detroit and see Belle before I go to the hospital. One cannot tell just how soon one can get out after an operation."

I said, "Yes, that is well. Go to Detroit." So she went to Detroit and had her visit with our oldest daughter, her husband and baby, and returned no better, but rather worse.

At this time it dawned on me that I had not in a definite way committed her to God. I had not received because I had not definitely asked. So I went to prayer and immediately the Holy Spirit said to me, "Have you confessed your faults?"

On reflecting, I said, "No."

Then He said, "You must confess your faults."

We were not living in an unkindly fashion, but there are many things in home lives which are not just as they ought to be. There were some of these things to my account and I acknowledged them. Then I went to pray, and I said, "Lord, You see that Your child is sick. We have been arranging for the hospital. You know that that takes time. It takes money. It involves danger; even the minor operations do not always result happily. You have the power; You can speak the word, if You will. Please help."

The next morning when I looked across to see her face, it

showed evident improvement. She was better in appearance than she had been for weeks. When she spoke she said, "I feel differently; I have not felt so well for a long time." So I thanked God, but I did not at that time tell her of my special prayer. Again, however, I asked God to perfect the work—to drive away the disease and make her well. The second morning she looked like a young woman, though she was about fifty years of age at that time. That disease left her as if it were a bird and had wings. It has never come near her since. She has had other ailments of one kind and another, but that particular disease has gone away. Some wise men tell me that her time had not come, that she would have recovered without prayer. I will not say that this is not true, for I am not a prophet; I am a witness.

I know that there was no improvement before the confession and prayer. I know that although she is a physician and is not given to special alarms, she felt afraid about herself, and I know that after I confessed my faults and prayed for her, God healed her, and so far as that trouble is concerned, she has been well ever since.

I give my testimony as it occurred and largely because of my own previous failures. When we confess our sins, God is faithful and just to forgive them. I hope there are very few who need to make confessions before they pray for the sick, but evidently some do or else James 5:16 would never have been written. The Holy Spirit says, "Confess your faults one to another, and pray one for another." If I had done it earlier, it would have saved me much, but I am glad I learned the lesson at last and that God helped me on that particular occasion to triumph through His grace.

An Infant Is Healed

The Bible clearly intimates that God bestows upon certain persons what are called "gifts of healing," upon others "pastoral gifts," upon others "teaching gifts." I was made a teacher, though certain other gifts in smaller measures have been bestowed upon me. I have never had nor aspired to gifts of healing, but I have desired to be helpful to sick and burdened people and I have at times prayed for them. No doubt many others did also, and I have seen most remarkable healings. For the encouragement of those who are called to pray for the sick, I would like to mention another instance.

One morning as I came into my office to begin my day's work, a lady, very much excited, came in and said that I was desired to go and pray in a home where an infant was dying. I said to her, "It is impossible for me to go at this time, but I will send a brother who can do so." And I asked the Rev. Mr. Hall, the assistant pastor of our church and a man of faith and of the Holy Spirit, to go in my stead. He did so, but returned after a time, saying that the family would be glad if I would come to the house. I went, stopping at our home on the way to take Mrs. Blanchard with me.

A gentleman opened the door of the house, and as he did so I asked him, "Are you the father of this child who is so ill?"

He said, "Yes."

I said to him, "Well, are you a Christian man?"

He answered, "Mr. Blanchard, I am a traveling man. You know how hard it is for a traveling man to be a Christian, but I do believe in God and I do believe in Jesus Christ and I try to be a Christian." I went on to the room where his wife was lying, herself just out of the hospital and very frail. She held my hand convulsively and sobbed bitterly as she said, "Mr. Blanchard, I say, 'Thy will be done.' You know how hard it is to say, 'Thy will be done,' but I do say it."

I went on into the next room. The little babe was lying on a pillow held in the lap of a neighbor. The doctor who had been attending him was sitting before him, his elbow on his knee, his chin resting in his hand, waiting to see the end. Already they had telephoned the nurse that it was unnecessary for her to come, that the baby was practically dead and she would be of no service. It was impossible for me to see a sign of life in the child. There was not a trace of color. I could not see the slightest movement of the lungs. If the child had been in a coffin, no one would have objected to burial, from anything which was obvious. But we prayed for the little fellow, and as I went back to the mother, I said, "I think that God will give you back your baby." At 5 o'clock that evening, I telephoned the house to know how the little one was getting on. The person who answered the phone said, "Baby is sleeping quietly. The pink has come back into his cheeks. We think he is getting well."

Three days later, as I was about to leave town, I phoned the house and the mother answered the phone. I asked, "How is the baby?"

She said: "He is very well—getting on nicely," and then she added, "People used to tell me that God does not work miracles in these days, but I know He does. He has worked one in this house."

I have no doubt whatever that what she said was literally true. Of course, God works miracles. The springtime is an uncounted host of miracles. We should be speechless with wonder, were it not that we are so accustomed to it.

A Railroad Engineer Testifies

A few weeks ago I was in the Eighth Avenue Mission in New York. On the platform by me sat a gentleman to whom I was introduced. When the meeting had progressed for an hour or so, Miss Wray, the superintendent, called on him for a testimony. He said, "Friends, about two and a half or three years ago I was in the hospital in Philadelphia. I was an engineer on the Pennsylvania Lines, and although I had a praying wife, I had all my life been a sinful man. At this time I was very ill. I became greatly wasted. I weighed less than 100 pounds. Finally the doctor who was attending me said to my wife that I was dead, but she said, 'No, he is not dead. He cannot be dead. I have prayed for him for twenty-seven years and God has promised me that he should be saved. Do you think God would let him die now after I have prayed twenty-seven years and God has promised, and he is not saved?' 'Well,' the doctor replied, 'I do not know anything about that, but I know that he is dead.' " And around my cot the screen was drawn—which in the hospital separates the living and the dead.

"To satisfy my wife, other physicians were brought, one after another, until seven were about the cot. Each one of them as he came up and made the examination confirmed the testimony of all who had preceded. The seven doctors said that I was dead. Meanwhile my wife was kneeling by the side of my cot, insisting that I was not dead—that if I were dead God would bring me back, for He had promised her that I should be saved and I was not yet saved. By and by her knees began to pain her, kneeling on the hard hospital floor. She asked the nurse for a pillow and the nurse brought her a pillow on which she kneeled. One hour, two hours, three hours passed. The screen still stood by the cot. I was lying there still, apparently dead. Four hours, five hours, six hours, seven hours, thirteen hours passed, and all this while my wife was kneeling by the cotside. When people remonstrated and wished her to go away she said, 'No, he has to be saved. God will bring him back if he is dead. He is not dead. He cannot die until he is saved.'

"At the end of thirteen hours I opened my eyes, and she asked, 'What do you wish, my dear?'

"And I answered, 'I wish to go home.'

"She said, 'You shall go home.'

"But when she proposed it, the doctors raised their hands in horror. They said, 'Why, it will kill him. It will be suicide.'

"She said, 'You have had your turn. You said he was dead already. I am going to take him home.'

"I now weigh 246 pounds. I still run a fast train on the Pennsylvania Lines. I have been out to Minneapolis on a little vacation, telling men what Jesus can do, and I am glad to tell you what Jesus can do."

I am absolutely certain that God is waiting to answer prayer—waiting to answer prayers for many. At times there are hindrances. Sometimes there are unconfessed faults. These are a deadly obstacle. Let us put them out of the way, so that we may pray one for another and see men healed.

We believe that one of the serious and most popular errors of the modern pulpit is the putting of more thought than prayer, of more head than of heart, in its sermons. Big hearts make big preachers; good hearts make good preachers. A theological school to enlarge and cultivate the heart is the gold desideratum of the Gospel. The pastor binds his people to him and rules his people by his heart. They may admire his gifts, they may be proud of his ability, they may be affected for the time by his sermons; but the stronghold of his power is his heart.

The Good Shepherd gives His life for the sheep. Heads never make martyrs. It is the heart which surrenders the life to love and fidelity. It takes great courage to be a faithful pastor, but the heart alone can supply this courage. Gifts and genius may be brave, but it is the gifts and genius of the heart and not of the head.

It is easier to fill the head than it is to prepare the heart. It is easier to make a brain sermon than a heart sermon. It was the heart that drew the Son of God from heaven. It is heart that will draw men to heaven. Men of heart is what the world needs to sympathize with its woe, to kiss away its sorrows, to compassionate its misery and to alleviate its pain. Christ was eminently the Man of sorrows, because He was preeminently the Man of heart. *E.M. Bounds*

CHAPTER TEN

ASK IN HIS NAME

Whatsoever ye shall ask in My name, that will I do" (John 14:13). This is another of those marvelous statements so broad and sweeping that they seem entirely too good to be true. Yet like all words of God, when we know exactly what they say and test them, we find them to be not partially, but literally and entirely according to fact. "Whatsoever ye shall ask in My name, that will I do."

I well remember when I first began to meditate on the expression, "In My name." I have thought of it a great deal since, have prayed about it some, though not so much as I should, and have studied it in the writings of others. I have been helped by meditation in answer to prayer and by the teaching of my brethren. Let me tell you what "In My name" means to me.

We Pray in His Name

If I draw a bank check and have no money in the bank, the bank will not pay me currency; but if I can secure an endorser who is known to the banker, who has money in the bank, who is a trustworthy man, then the bank will let me have the money. If I ask in my own name I do not receive. If I ask in the name of my friend who is able, I do receive.

If I pray in the name of Jesus—that is, if I request things from God, relying upon His power, His merits—I am asking in His name. If I make these same requests, relying upon my own merits, upon my own worth or works, then I am asking in my own name and I have no promise. In the former case I have. "If ye shall ask anything *in My name*, I will do it" (John 14:14). "That whatsoever ye shall ask of the Father *in My name*, He may give it you" (John 15:16).

We are so prone to close our prayers with words like these, "For Jesus' sake," or something equivalent. This is all right, provided we know what we are saying and mean what we say. But how many times, repeating these solemn words, do we actually have in mind for the sake of Jesus, because of His worth and work? Often we say, "For Jesus' sake," without thinking what it means, or hoping to receive because of what we are, have done, or may yet do.

The most effective illustration of asking in the name of another came to me years ago: It was during the Civil War and a gentleman in Indianapolis had an only son who enlisted in the armies of the Union. The father was a banker and though he consented to his son's going, it seemed as if it would take his very life to have him go. He was ceaselessly interested in soldiers. Whenever he saw a uniform, his heart went out to it as he thought of his boy. Neglecting his business he spent his time and gave his money for raising companies or regiments, for caring for soldiers invalided home. At last his friends remonstrated, "There ought to be moderation in all things. You have no right to neglect your business in this manner." And he resolved that he would not spend so much time and thought upon soldiers, that he would attend to his business and let the government take care of the boys in blue.

After he had come to this decision, there stepped into his bank one day a private soldier in a faded, worn uniform, who showed in his face and hands the marks of the hospital. The poor fellow was fumbling in his shirt to get something or other, when the banker saw him and, perceiving his purpose, said to him, "I cannot do anything for you today. I am extremely busy. You will have to go up to headquarters; the officers there will look after you."

Still the poor convalescent stood, not seeming fully to understand what was said to him. Still he fumbled in his shirt and by and by fished out a scrap of dirty paper, on which were a few lines written in pencil, and laid it before the banker. On it were written these words:

Dear Father,
This is one of my comrades. He was wounded in our last fight and has been in the hospital. Please receive him as myself.

Charlie

In a moment all the resolutions of indifference which this man had made flew away. He took the boy to his palatial home, put him into Charlie's room, gave him Charlie's seat at the table, kept him until food and rest and love had brought him back to life, and then sent him back again to peril his life for the flag. The boy asked in Charlie's name and the father responded to his request.

We May Offend God
No man ever comes to God with such a reliance on Jesus Christ as that soldier lad had on the plea of his comrade, and is sent away unhelped. "If ye shall ask anything in My name, I will do it." We are terribly prone to self-conceit, to self-righteousness, to dependence on the human in some way, and God is not pleased with this and does not make answer. He wishes us to come in the name of His Son. Jesus Christ left His throne in heaven, the songs of the angels, the sights of the crystal rivers, the never-dying trees, and the shining walls, to live in a laborer's cottage, to be rejected and despised by the creatures He had made, and finally to be publicly executed as a criminal, not for His own ill-doing but for ours. "He was wounded for our transgressions, He was bruised for our iniquities; the chastisement of our peace was upon Him; and with His stripes we are healed" (Isa. 53:5).
What an offense, what an indignity when all this has been done for us, for us to proffer requests at the throne of heaven because of our own little righteousnesses, which are in the sight of God like filthy rags. God cannot answer such petitions. They offend Him. If we mean better than we pray, and our ignorances lead us to such blundering, He will forgive us; but He is not pleased and this is not the road to successful prayer. Praying in the name of Jesus is praying in order that the name of Jesus may be glorified,

His kingdom built up, His church established. This test causes many of our supposed prayers to disappear.

Why We Pray

My child is sick. I am worn with watching, tired out, and I pray for the healing of my child. Why? In order that Jesus Christ may be glorified? In order that other sick people may hear what a great Saviour Jesus Christ is, and coming to Him obtain help which they may testify to others, thus passing on the word to the glory of God?

Not at all. I am likely to pray in order that my doctor's bills may cease to accumulate, so that I may be able to sleep nights, that I may not be distressed by the sight of pain which I cannot relieve, so that my boy may get back to his place in the school, and that he may help about the work at home.

There are a thousand reasons for which I may pray apart from the honor of Jesus, but if I do not pray that He may be glorified—only that I may be eased and comforted—what object would He have in answering my prayer?

God is very merciful to our ignorances, and when we mean better than we do He knows it; but the promise is definitely made to those who ask in the name of Jesus. If we do not ask in His name, we have not a promise to rely on, though in His mercy He may go beyond His promise and aid us without desert. But I write for serious people who really wish to know how to pray, who wonder why their prayers have not been more prevailing, who would like to pray prevailingly, and so I state this condition as it is in the Word of God. If we are to succeed in prayer, we must pray in the name of Jesus. This means that there are two things we desire—first, that God may grant our petitions because we come in the name of Jesus, relying on the merits of Jesus, having no confidence in our own righteousness; and, second, that Jesus may be glorified, that people may hear of the wonderful things that He does, and thus hearing, repent, believe, and receive blessing. This it is, I think, to ask in the name of Jesus and His is an all-prevailing name.

When a Christian does not yield entirely to the leading of the Spirit—and this is certainly the will of God and the work of His grace—he lives, without knowing it, under the power of "the flesh." This life of "the flesh" manifests itself in many different ways. It appears in the hastiness of spirit, or the anger which so unexpectedly arises in you, in the lack of love for which you have so often blamed yourself; in the pleasure found in eating and drinking, about which at times your conscience has chidden you; in that seeking for your own will and honor, that confidence in your own wisdom and power, that pleasure in the world, of which you are sometimes ashamed before God. All this is life "after the flesh." "Ye are yet carnal" (1 Cor. 3:3)—that text, perhaps, disturbs you at times; you have not full peace and joy in God.

I pray you take time and give an answer to the question:—Have I not found here the cause of my prayerlessness, of my powerlessness to effect any change in the matter? I live in the Spirit, I have been born again, but I do not walk after the Spirit—"the flesh" lords it over me. The carnal life cannot possibly pray in the spirit and power. God forgive me. The carnal life is evidently the cause of my sad and shameful prayerlessness. *Andrew Murray*

CHAPTER ELEVEN

ASK ACCORDING
TO HIS WILL

We are speaking of the
conditions of successful prayer. In this matter, as in all others which are of life-and-death importance, the teaching of God's Word is so plain that he may "run that readeth it" (Hab. 2:2). "The wayfaring men, though fools, shall not err therein" (Isa. 35:8). "And this is the confidence that we have in Him, that, if we ask anything according to His will, He heareth us; and if we know that He hear us, whatsoever we ask, we know that we have the petitions that we desired of Him" (1 John 5:14-15).

But how can we be sure that we are asking according to the will of God, the will of Jesus Christ? Can we be sure? Or must we wait for the end and finally learn that we have or have not asked according to His will? I used to be greatly troubled about this matter. How many times I prayed and still was in doubt as to the will of God. By and by I was compelled to act. The time for deliberation was past and I had to move. Often having done so and having reached the end of a passage in my life, I could look back, as John Bunyan did over the path he had traversed, and I could see that God had guided me as I asked Him to, had upheld, protected, energized.

One time I said to my father, "I wish I could know *when I act*, whether I am doing according to the will of God or not. I pray according to James 1:5: 'Lord, I lack wisdom. I desire wisdom. Please give me wisdom,' and yet I am not sure that He has done so. I go forward into the dark. After a time I can see that my prayer has been answered, that God has given me wisdom, that I have desired things which were according to His will, but I wish I might know it at the time."

My father said to me, "You need Proverbs 16:3: 'Commit thy works unto the Lord, and thy thoughts shall be established.' "

Your Thoughts Established

What is it to have your thoughts established? It is to feel sure respecting the thing that you are thinking of. If your thoughts are established when you are asking for guidance, you will be settled in a conviction that you are being guided. You shall know that God is keeping His word to you.

The Old Testament Prophet Balaam did not have his thoughts established because his works were not committed to God. His difficulty was that he wanted the reward which the king of Moab could give him. He prayed to God to know if he should go to see the king.

God said, "No, do not go." The king's messengers came back, promising larger rewards, and he asked God again whether he should go. He knew what God wished, but he wished something else. Balaam loved the *wages* of unrighteousness even though he did not love the unrighteousness. He wanted the things that the king could give him. Yet he was afraid to go against the commands of God. Balaam's ways were not committed to the Lord. He could not say as David did, "I delight to do Thy will, O my God" (Ps. 40:8). Yet in a way, Balaam did obey the will of God. He did not go to the king until he was permitted and then he said the things he was required to say. But he did not delight in the will of God. (See Numbers 22—24.)

When we commit our ways to Him, He establishes our thoughts; that is, He teaches us the things that He wills for us to be and do. Guidance of this kind makes life beautiful; to be without it is not only sorrow but can be a deadly danger as well.

Here, for example, is a young man who is attracted by a bright, beautiful, gifted young woman. He is a Christian man. She is a very lovely woman of the world. When he asks God for success in his wooing, the Spirit says to him, "You are a Christian and she is not a Christian. You will be unequally joined if you are married. You are a child of God. She belongs to the world." If this man's works are committed to God, if he is willing to go God's way, if he is willing to marry her or anybody else, or not to marry at all, just as God shall plan, he can receive certain guidance. In this particular instance, God has spoken in His Word. He reinforces His Word by His Spirit. In some instances He speaks by His prophets and by His Spirit, but always He speaks. No one commits his work to God honestly and entirely without being able to ask according to the will of Jesus.

A ministerial brother told me that a young lady, a member of his church, once came to him and said, "Pastor, I am to be married next week, on Wednesday. I wish you would come around to our house in the evening and perform the ceremony."

He asked, "Are you to marry this young man with whom you have been keeping company?"

"Yes."

"Well, I cannot marry you."

She was greatly surprised and asked, "Why not?"

"Because you are a child of God and he is a man of the world, and I am forbidden to marry you."

"Well," she said, "I think it very strange if my pastor will not marry me."

He said, "I will gladly marry you if you will marry in the Lord. But I will not take the reponsibility of joining you in marriage to a man who is not a Christian."

It was not difficult for her to find a minister who had no such scruples. She was married according to program. Within a year she was a heartbroken bride and came to her pastor, "O Pastor, if I had only known—if I had only known." She might more properly have said, "If I had only obeyed," for she did know. What she lacked was a disposition to obey.

A Christian man once said to me that he had just finished paying $150,000 of security money. I said to him, "Why did you do that? You had no right to do so, being a Christian."

"Why not?"

"Because the Word of God forbids you to do things of that kind."

"There is nothing about that in the Bible."

"Oh, yes, there is plenty about that in the Bible. 'Be not thou one of them that strike hands, or of them that are sureties for debts' " (Prov. 22:26).

"Well," he said, "I have been a Bible teacher ever since I was a young man and I supposed I knew the Bible pretty well, but I never knew there was anything in it about going a security. If I had obeyed that verse it would have saved me $150,000."

I had a friend who was a banker and also an earnest Christian. He had a brother who was not a confessed Christian, who had been a Spiritualist and a Christian Scientist. This brother came to my friend and said to him, "I would like to put $50,000 into your bank and be a partner with you."

My friend answered, "No, brother, that will not do."

"Why not?"

"Because I am a Christian and you are not a Christian. If we were partners we should inevitably quarrel. We would become hard in our feelings one toward the other. You would want to look over the books or work on Sunday, and I would not permit it, and then you would find fault and I should find fault and there would be trouble. I tell you what you do. There is a good building two blocks below us. Buy that building and take out a charter for a national bank. I will help you every way I can. If any of my depositors wish to go to you I will encourage them to do it. In this way you and I can continue friends, as we always have been. If we should be partners, we should not be friends. We cannot afford to sacrifice our friendship as brothers for a little money."

How wise men would be if they would simply give attention to what God says. Of course, in order to give attention to it they must know what it is. Here is oftentimes the failure. Men read the Bible in streaks or spots. They do not read it as a whole. The result may be that the very teaching which they require for the particular emergency which is upon them, they do not have. They ask but do not ask according to the mind of Jesus, according to the will of God; and of course, unless God grants their petitions as a matter of discipline and punishment, they cannot receive the things which they desire.

In my own experience I can truly say that since my father gave me Proverbs 16:3, I have never patiently waited on God for wisdom with my works fully committed, willing and determined to do according to the mind of God, without knowing that He willed the thing which I decided to do.

The Peril of Haste

Apart from self-determination in this matter, I think the next great danger is haste. "He that hasteth with his feet sinneth" (Prov. 19:2); "He that believeth shall not make haste" (Isa. 28:16). In other words, if we wish to ask according to His will, we must take time to find out what His will is, and we must take as much time as is necessary. God does not permit us to rush into His presence and to give Him orders, to tell Him that we have very little time to spend with Him, and that He must answer us immediately. All such dealing is an offense to God. As I have said before, He is very patient with us when He knows that our hearts are right. He makes allowance for temperamental conditions. He knows when we blunder because we are willful, and when we blunder because we are defective.

I heard Dr. Herrick Johnson once say in an address to theological students, "My young brethren, never go into a pulpit unless you are sure you have something to say which is true. Men have doubts enough of their own and the preaching of doubts is never a good thing for anybody—for the man who preaches or for those who listen. But when you are certain that you have a message from God that men need, you can preach with confidence and power and God will bless it. This will limit your field somewhat; but you will find that there are plenty of things in the Christian faith which you can know are true, about which you need have no doubt whatsoever. Those are the things which you should preach."

What he said to those young ministers I would say to every child of God who reads these words. You do not need to be in a hurry. You will find the old proverb true, "The more haste, the less speed." When I was a boy I read a story which was very instructive and helpful.

A young man, starting out on horseback for a certain city, met an old man and said to him, "I am riding for such a town. Do you think I will get there by night?"

The elderly man replied, "Yes, you may if you ride slow enough." The young man thought this was a most ridiculous reply and, using spur and whip, he hurried along the way as fast as he could go.

After a little while his horse was worn out and could not travel so well. By this time his old friend whom he had left behind, overtook him and the young man asked again, "Do you think I shall get to this town by nightfall?"

The elder man said, "Yes, if you ride fast enough." But he could not ride fast enough. He had exhausted his animal in the unseemly haste of the morning hours and he was compelled to journey in the darkness, while his friend who had given him good counsel and had set him a good example, was safely housed by the time the sun was down. This little story contains truth which every thoughtful person may well heed. He that believeth will not make haste.

God is willing to teach us His will. If we wait on Him obediently, He will do it. If we are disobedient, or if we are in disrespectful haste, we must go without guidance and fare as we can.

I once heard Mr. Moody preaching about salvation. He remarked that some men claim that their nervous systems have been so injured by wrong living, that it is impossible for them to become really saved. Mr. Moody replied to them, "If God can make the world, it is certainly a small affair for Him to make a new set of nerves for a man who is willing to do what is right and desires to be saved." We are not hindered in our prayers by any unwillingness or inabililty on the part of God. We are hindered by our own defects and failures. If we ask according to the will of God, He hears us.

It is possible for us to know what His will is and it is

possible for us to ask according to it. If we fail to do this, we ought not to complain of unanswered prayer, for prayer which does not comply with the clearly expressed conditions is not prayer at all. It is an attempt to coax God to do things which He has said He will not do. This is not praying—it is insulting God.

"Why, then," said the minister, "do you not try this again? As you go to your inner chamber, however cold and dark your heart may be, do not try in your own might to force yourself into the right attitude. Bow before Him, and tell Him that He sees in what a sad state you are, and that your only hope is in Him. Trust Him, with a childlike trust, to have mercy upon you, and wait upon Him. In such a trust you are in a right relationship to Him. You have nothing— He has everything." Some time later she told the minister that his advice had helped her; she had learned that faith in the love of the Lord Jesus is the only method of getting into fellowship with God in prayer.

Do you not begin to see, my reader, that there are two kinds of warfare—the first when we seek to conquer prayerlessness in our own strength. In that case, my advice to you is:—"Give over your restlessness and effort; fall helpless at the feet of the Lord Jesus; He will speak the word, and your soul will live." If you have done this, then, second, comes the message—This is but the beginning of everything. It will require deep earnestness, and the exercise of all your power, and a watchfulness of the entire heart—eager to detect the least backsliding. Above all, it will require a surrender to a life of self-sacrifice that God really desires to see in us and which He will work out for us. *Andrew Murray*

CHAPTER TWELVE

FAITH IN GOD

Faith is another of the clearly expressed conditions of successful prayer. "Without faith it is impossible to please Him, for he that cometh to God *must* believe that He is, and that He is a rewarder of them that diligently seek Him" (Heb. 11:6). It is said that a lad, being asked what faith is, replied, "Faith is believing things that are not true." Of course, this answer may be all right for a boy. But do not a great many adults also have an ill-defined feeling that this is about the sum of the matter?

I read a definition of faith which I like very much: "Faith is a disposition to believe what is true, upon sufficient evidence." Someone has said, "Faith is confidence impersonated." One of the words which we often use as equivalent to faith is trust. When I say that I have faith in a man, I simply mean that I trust him. In our dealings with God, we shall often obtain help if we remember that we are made in His likeness. This means in His spiritual likeness, for God is a Spirit and those who worship Him must worship Him in spirit and in truth. If we are spiritually created in the image of God, then barring sin and the effects of sin, we may expect to find in our own being hints and suggestions as to His. If exercising faith in a man is trusting him, exercising faith in God is trusting God.

When I trust a man, what do I do? I believe what he tells me and that he will fulfill the promises he makes. If I say that I trust him and do not expect him to keep his word or do not rely upon what he has said, I am telling a lie. It is just so with God. Trusting God is believing, expecting that

He will keep His word, that what He says is true, is according to fact. With this test in mind, it will be perfectly easy for men to know whether they have faith in Him or not. God says, for example, that it shall be well with the righteous and ill with the wicked. Do you believe this to be fact? God declares that He will receive the righteous into glorious habitations and punish the wicked in the pool of fire. Do you believe this to be true? God says that if we commit our works to Him, our thoughts shall be established. Do you believe this to be true? He says that if we ask, we shall receive; if we seek, we shall find; that if we knock, the door shall be opened. Do you believe this to be true? I am afraid that many persons say they have faith in God because they know they ought to trust Him, when in fact they do not. This is a dangerous situation.

The Importance of Trust

It is remarkable how men enjoy being trusted. How many times I have seen the good son or daughter of a good parent brighten when the father or mother says, "I can trust my boy or girl." Many times tears fill the eyes of the children. They are so glad that their parents confide in them. And parents are just as pleased when their children rely, without doubt or hesitation, on their word.

I read years ago of a father whose son was away at school. Coming home for a brief vacation, he was going over the estate with his father. While looking at a wall which was standing on the land, the father remarked to the boy that he intended to have that wall taken down.

The lad said, "Father, I would like to see it taken down. Will you let me be here when it is taken down?"

The father replied, "Yes, my boy, I will."

The lad returned to his school life and the father, in the rush of affairs, forgot his promise and had the wall removed while the boy was away. When the lad returned, he said, "Father, you told me that I might see that wall taken down."

The father replied, "Yes, my boy, I did. I forgot. I am sorry, but you shall see a wall taken down, though I forgot my promise."

He called for laborers and had the wall re-erected. Then he had it removed while his boy looked on. A neighbor said to him, "You are a born fool. You have spent one hundred pounds for the whim of a child."

But the wise father replied, "I wish my children to know that I keep my word with them, if it costs me everything I am worth in this world."

God is pleased when we trust Him, and the more simple and unquestioning our confidence, the more gratified He is. It is impossible to please Him without faith, but faith pleases Him wonderfully.

Mr. Moody's Prayer Answered

During D.L. Moody's campaign of the World's Fair year (1893), Moody had need of $3,000. Things were very pressing and his need at that time was imperative. Moody knelt down by the desk in his room at the Bible Institute in Chicago and prayed, "Lord, You know I need $3,000 today— that I must have it, and You know that I am too busy with Your work to go out and get it. Please send it to me. I thank You that You will. Amen."

Mr. Moody then rose and went out about his work. Later he was to preach in the Auditorium. The audience had assembled and the platform was filled. A young woman came up to an usher and said, "I wish to see Mr. Moody."

"You cannot see Mr. Moody. The meeting is about to begin."

"But I must see Mr. Moody."

"You cannot see Mr. Moody." She went around to another aisle and tried a different usher, with the same result. She then went around to the stage entrance and found her way past the usher who thought her to be a singer. She worked her way down to the front and put an envelope into Mr. Moody's hand. He crushed it into his vest pocket, and went on with his meeting.

At dinner, remembering he had received a letter at the meeting, he took it out of his pocket, and found it to contain a check for $3,000. This was the answer to his prayer. He afterward learned that that morning a Christian woman said to herself, "These are busy days for Mr. Moody. He must require a great deal of money" and she made out a check for $1,000. After she had written it, the Spirit said to her, "That will not be sufficient. He will need more money than that." So she tore it up and made out a check of $2,000. This did not seem to satisfy. Since she still felt sure that it was not sufficient, she destroyed the slip of paper and wrote another for $3,000, called her maid and said, "Will you please put this in the postbox over there?" But just as the maid was about to leave the room, she said, "He may not get it until tomorrow and he may need it today. Put on your things and slip over to the Auditorium. Give it to Mr. Moody, and do not let anyone else have it." So the Spirit of God responds to the faith of man.

If we ask anything according to His will, He hears us, and if we know that He hears us, we know that we have the things that we desire of Him. When we know that, of course we believe. We believe Him in general and we believe Him in particular. We trust for the special thing at hand and we trust Him for all the things which are to come. Without faith it is impossible to please Him, and faith is not so much an intellectual state as a disposition. It is the loving heart of a child going out in confidence to the loving care of a father. It is not strange that faith works such wonders and it is not strange that God is so offended with those who will not believe.

George Müller's Case

Perhaps there has been no greater example of triumphant faith than of George Müller, the Bristol orphanage man. I count it one of the great blessings of my life to have seen and heard him, for such men are very rare in the history of the church. At times he had over 2,000 persons to feed and clothe and shelter. It was with him, as with J. Hudson Taylor of the China Inland Mission, a fixed principle not to go in debt for anything. It was also with each of these brothers a fixed principle not to make requests directly of men, but only of God. They never appealed to men respecting the Lord's work and they trusted the Holy Spirit to use the Word to incite them to the work which God would have them do.

At one time Mr. Müller was planning for the erection of a large building. It was to cost some $75,000. After he prayed for a time, a first gift came in from England, another from Australia, and other gifts followed until he had in hand over $60,000. One of his friends said, "We ought to begin putting up the building. God has given so much, He will certainly give the rest."

But Mr. Müller said, "No. God is in as great a hurry for that building as I am. He knows what it is for and He knows where to get the money with which to put it up. We will not lay a brick or disturb a shovelful of earth until the money is in the bank." They did not, and when the building was complete, it is said that there remained a small balance over and above the expenses of construction.

What an example this is to many of us who have often-times been in greater haste about God's work than He was, and who have therefore come into all sorts of difficulties. I myself heard Mr. Müller say that during his life in the orphanages, he had not simply scores of times, but literally hundreds of times, been absolutely destitute of food and money when a meal for his great family was finished. "And yet," he said, "in all these years, never on a single occasion has God permitted those orphans to go without a meal at the time when it was due. In order to provide for them, He has literally sent money from all the ends of the earth, awakened people out of sleep, sent people out of their way, done seemingly almost everything that could be done to make sure that those who were trusting Him should not lack for any good thing."

Faith as a Grain of Mustard Seed

One of the verses on prayer which has been a great comfort and help to me is the word of our Lord, "If ye have faith as a grain of mustard seed, ye shall say unto this mountain, 'Remove hence to yonder place;' and it shall remove; and nothing shall be impossible unto you" (Matt. 17:20). I think this verse was intended to be a help to those who are conscious of defective faith. Jesus' disciples were asking that He should give them more faith. He seemed to tell them that they should use what they had. Is not this a part of the divine plan?

Many times when I have realized that my faith was far less than it ought to be, I have said to God, "Father, I have not the faith which I ought to have, but do I not have faith like a grain of mustard seed?" And it has seemed to me that He always has said, "Yes," and has granted me that thing which I desired.

Faith in a person depends always upon knowledge of his characteristics, and knowledge of characteristics is gained by acquaintance. If I wish to know what sort of a man one is, I need to associate with him, to hear what he says, to see what he does. If I become acquainted with God, learn what His character is, it will be natural for me to trust Him, for He is trustworthy. Acquaintance with the unreliable, uncertain, untruthful, breeds doubt. We do not trust such persons even when they say what is true or do what is right. But persons of integrity, of character, of righteousness—these people always awaken faith when we come to know them. As we do what the Word says and acquaint ourselves with God, we shall be at peace with Him.

What we have said about deliverance from the sin of prayerlessness has also application, as answer, to the question: "How may the experience of deliverance be maintained?" Redemption is not granted to us piecemeal, or as something of which we may make use from time to time. It is bestowed as a fullness of grace stored up in the Lord Jesus, which may be enjoyed in a new fellowship with Him every day. It is so necessary that this great truth should be driven home and fastened in our minds, that I will once more mention it. Nothing can preserve you from carelessness, or make it possible for you to persevere in living, powerful prayer, but a daily close fellowship with Jesus our Lord.

He said to His disciples: "Ye believe in God, believe also in Me. . . .Believe Me that I am in the Father, and the Father in Me. . . .He that believeth on Me, the works that I do shall he do also, and greater works than these shall he do" (John 14:1, 11-12).

The Lord wished to teach His disciples that all they had learned from the Old Testament concerning the power and holiness and love of God must now be transferred to Him. They must not believe merely in certain written documents, but in Him personally. They must believe that He was in the Father, and the Father in Him, in such a sense that they had one life, one glory. All that they knew about Christ, they would find in God. *Andrew Murray*

CONSTANCY
IN PRAYER

He spake a parable unto them to this end, that men ought always to pray, and not to faint" (Luke 18:1). It is in the duty of perseverance where many of us break down. God oftentimes delays answers to prayer because He wishes us to learn to trust Him in the dark, to believe when we cannot see. Do not earthly parents do the same? Who is there who is wise with his children who has not at times waited to bestow some good gift which he had already willed, in order that his children might learn to confide?

What difference can it make to the Almighty whether He bestows a good gift upon me at one time or another? God's resources are infinite; so also is His wisdom and love. That He does delay, we all know. I have had friends who said, "I do not think we ought to ask God for the same thing repeatedly. He knows whether something is best for us to have or not. He will surely do what is best. Why not, therefore, simply remind Him of our need and then wait?" The objection to this teaching is that it is contrary to the word of Jesus Christ on the same subject.

In Luke 11, our Lord is giving particular instructions in regard to prayer. He deals with this very question of repetition in verses 5 to 13, and clearly intimates that on men who persevere in prayer God will bestow good gifts which He will not bestow on people who do not persevere in prayer. The man in the story came to his neighbor for

85

bread. It was inconvenient to supply it and the neighbor declined; but because of his importunity, he rose and gave him as many as he needed (Luke 11:8). Jesus went on to say, "Ask, and it shall be given you; seek, and ye shall find." I think it is not by accident that He unites the prayer of importunity with the promise to prayer.

In one of our church prayer meetings, a lady rose and said, "My father is a drunkard. I have prayed seven years that God would save him and he is not saved. It seems as if God did not hear or did not care, and I am discouraged. I do not know what to do."

She had only taken her seat when a lady rose and said, "My father was a drunkard fifteen years and I prayed for him all through those years. Then he was saved, not alone from drink but from all other sins. Now for fifteen years he has been a happy Christian. I think my sister ought not to be discouraged, but to pray on." This instance was very impressive because of the two testimonies which came one after the other.

I once heard Mr. Müller say in Chicago, "I have prayed for two men by name every day for thirty-five years; on land or sea, sick or well, I have remembered them before God by name, requesting their salvation. They are both living; they are neither of them saved, but I shall continue to pray for them daily, by name, until they are saved, or they die."

His biographer later wrote that at about the time of Müller's death, two persons for whom Mr. Müller had prayed for sixty-two years were converted. Here was a man praying every day for sixty-two years for the salvation of two men. At the end of that time they were saved. What a lesson that is for us. What a reproof for our lack of perseverance. What an encouragement to continue in prayer. "Men ought always to pray, and not to faint."

A Gradual Answer

North of our Wheaton College campus there stood an old frame building. It was not particularly valuable in itself, but the land on which it stood was very valuable. One of our honored trustees, Dr. R.J. Bennett, purchased the house and the land and gave them to the College. This bit of land constituted about one-third of the block of which it was a part. Two-thirds remained. One portion of this was owned in New York, the other in Nebraska. It was obvious to anyone who looked at the land situation, that the possession of that strip would be very helpful to the College.

I asked the owners to give it to the College. They declined to do so. I repeated the request after an interval of years and still they felt that it was more than they could do. At last I began to pray that the Lord would give us the land. At times I left the sidewalk and stood upon the ground, reminding myself that God had promised Jacob what the soles of his feet trod upon. I reminded God of this same promise and, as well as I could, claimed by faith this land for the College. Still it did not come. Years passed into other years. It was good ground, beautifully located. It would have been a very pleasant place for residences, yet there it lay, unoccupied.

Finally, the parties who owned the New York strip directed their agent to make sale. He put it on the market, intending to force the sale for what he could get. Special assessments were high, and were to be increased. I asked the owner, "What will you let us have that land for?" He said, "For $2,000."

I went to a generous friend who had made us debtor many times, and said to her, "For about $2,000 we can secure this property which is admirably located, and which we really need."

She at once said, "I think I can furnish the money within a few months." She did and that portion of the land came into our possession.

Still there was the remaining one-third which lay between the other two. The parties who owned it now wished to sell it and I desired it for the College. I thanked God many times for the two pieces which He had given and asked Him for the third piece. Nobody bought it. Finally the owner made us a proposition, which, without the expenditure of any money on our part, would enable us to secure the land. It is now a part of the college possession, not for our own uses but for the instruction of young people through all the years until the Lord comes, and for a part in His work during the millennial years.

Delayed Answers

The most remarkable instance of delayed answers to prayer which has come to my attention was suggested by Mr. Moody in a sermon he preached many years ago. He reminded us that when Moses was praying for the privilege of going over Jordan into the Promised Land, the Lord did not tell him that he could not go to the Promised Land. He said to him when the request was pressed, "Speak no more unto Me of this matter" (Deut. 3:26). That was not a refusal—that was a direction. Fifteen hundred years later, Moses was in the Holy Land with Elijah, talking with our Lord about the work which He was to accomplish at Jerusalem. He did not cross over Jordan, as God told him he would not. He did go into the Holy Land, as he prayed that he might, but he went by way of heaven.

It is so wonderful to think that God should keep the prayer of Moses before Him all those 1,500 years. When He was to send down to the Mount of Transfiguration two redeemed ones to talk with His Son about the death which He was to die for their sins and for the sins of the whole world, He selected Moses and Elijah. It is my firm conviction that if the Lord's people would inquire among their friends who are spiritually minded, they would be astounded at the number of cases in which God has answered prayer after long delay. As I have said before, this has not just *happened* so and it is not the result of any inability on the part of God. He can work His own will at His own pleasure and in His own time.

I heard the president of a university once say that God could use foolish people to accomplish His purpose, but that He never did so voluntarily. I was startled as I thought of the words of the Bible, *"God hath chosen* the foolish things of the world to confound the wise; and *God hath chosen* the weak things of the world to confound the things which are mighty; and base things of the world, and things which are despised, *hath God chosen*, yea, and things which are not, to bring to nought things that are" (1 Cor. 1:27-28)

God does choose the instruments which He uses. He does not take them from necessity, but because of His own choice. And God does not answer prayer after fifteen hundred years, or after seven years, or after fifteen years, or after sixty-two years because He could not answer in as many months if it pleased Him. There is a reason for delay.

It is safe to say that in a majority of instances of long delay, God has a number of purposes to accomplish. In the first place, it is a test of our own faith and obedience. He tells us always to pray and not to faint. Delays in answers to prayer are one means of testing us to know whether we can do this or not. It is also a wonderful confirmation of faith when the answer does come. If I receive a gift, after praying for it for ten years, my mind is impressed very differently from what it would be if I received the same gift after praying only ten minutes.

We shall never understand God's dealings with us here unless we remember that we come into the kingdom of God as babes and that He has to educate us, train us, raise us precisely as parents have to train, educate, raise children. We are children and He is our Father. He is the Creator of our bodies, but He is the Father of our souls, and He wishes us to be strong and pure and holy and useful, just as any good father wishes his children to be. To this end He disciplines, and one of the ways in which He disciplines is by delaying answers to prayer.

God Takes No Instructions

I was in New York some years ago, calling on an old friend who had been at Knox College during my father's presidency there. In an adjoining room lay his sick daughter, near to death. I had prayer with her and was glad that God seemed to show mercies to her in her poor, wrecked and tormented body. For some little time it looked as if she might recover, though I do not believe this was the plan of God. The next year when I was in New York I found that she had died. A friend who was intimate with the family told me something that was very terrible about her dying. A friend came to the room, prayed for her and said, "God, You have promised to answer prayer and we have complied with all the conditions. We command You to heal this sick one." I did not wonder that she died; I wondered that the person who offered the prayer did not die. Except that she was ignorant and God could pardon her, it seemed to me that He would certainly have struck her dead then and there. God does not permit us to give Him orders.

> He sits on no precarious throne,
> nor borrows leave to be.

And He does not wish to have people say that they command Him. I do not think that He cares to hear us say that we have complied with all the conditions of successful prayer. I am certain that when we do, He knows it and is satisfied. But He does not require us to tell Him that since we have complied with the conditions, it is time for Him to fulfill His word. This seems a frightful blasphemy and I hope that none of the Lord's children who read these words will ever be guilty of so offending against the Majesty of heaven. A sensible person proferring a request to an earthly monarch would never think of doing so in such insulting and outrageous terms. Is it not strange that our brothers and sisters can sometimes insult God by addressing Him as they would never dare to speak to a human being?

Trusting God

When George Müller was telling us about praying for those two men for thirty-five years, he also said that the first two men he spoke with in the name of Jesus, after his own conversion, were very quickly saved. At first they laughed when he spoke to them on the subject. He went into his bedroom adjacent, fell on his knees and with tears begged God to save those two young men. When he came out, they were both of them ready to submit to God. He said that he received the impression that everybody he spoke to or prayed for would be immediately converted. When he began to pray one year, two years, three years, four years, five years, for the same person, with no apparent result, he was surprised and a bit disheartened. But he reflected that God's promise was not to answer in five minutes, or five years, or fifty years, but to answer. That it was his part to believe and to continue making request, and that if he did this, God would certainly fulfill His part of the contract. He said, "I lost the feeling of disappointment which I had had and was encouraged to lay hold on God patiently, perseveringly, every day until the answer came."

In this connection I think it is helpful to remember about our Lord's praying in Gethsemane. He prayed once, He prayed twice, He prayed the third time, and it is interesting to note in speaking of these repeated petitions, that the Word says, "saying the same words" (Matt. 26:44). How can one reconcile this fact with the teaching of some who say that when we have once proffered a petition, it is an exhibition of distrust or rebellious spirit if we make the same request again. I do not believe that this is true. Had it been, certainly our Lord Jesus Christ would never have prayed three times, saying the same words each time. The fact is that we must be taught by the Spirit how to pray. Sometimes He will teach us to pray once and to look upon the transaction as completed. Sometimes He will bid us pray more than once and when He does so, we must persevere in prayer. "Men ought always to pray, and not to faint."

My father once visited a dying pastor in the city of Cincinnati. The dying man had great difficulty in speaking, in fact could scarcely speak at all. My father asked him if he would like him to pray, and he nodded his head affirmatively. My father said to him, "Shall I pray for your wife and children?" and he shook his head negatively, and then gathering up what strength he had, said, "Yesterday I prayed for them." Yesterday he had closed that transaction with God and he did not wish to reopen it. He had prayed for those dear people once; he knew God had heard him and would answer in due time. In his bodily frailty his faith was strong, and he did not care to pray twice when be believed he already had the answer of God.

Years ago I was very much burdened for a friend. I prayed repeatedly that the Lord would do a certain thing for that friend. At last it seemed to me that God said to me by His Spirit, "You leave that matter with Me and I will take care of it." I did so. I have never prayed that prayer since, so far as I know. Sometimes I have thought of doing so and have almost begun to pray and then it has come to me that that is a completed transaction between God and me. So I have stopped and thanked Him that He has accepted my petition, that He would answer my prayer, and I have left that matter definitely in His hands. It is blessed to do so and from time to time remind Him that He has promised and that I know He will fulfill my petition in His own time.

I have had that same experience about erecting buildings. I have thanked God for them; I have seen them in my mind fully completed, standing fair and beautiful on the ground, when not a shovelful of earth has been turned, when not a brick or stone has been laid.

If I am speaking to those who have been burdened because of unanswered prayer, and I do not doubt there are some such among those who will read these pages, let me encourage you. There is no such thing as unanswered prayer in this world, but there are prayers the answers to which are long delayed. It is well that it is so. It would harm us if it were otherwise. If you will be victoriously patient, you will be victoriously successful in your praying.

PART THREE

WHY DOES GOD ANSWER PRAYER?

How little this is understood by Christians! How many there are who allow themselves to be misled, and rest satisfied with the thought that sin is a necessity, that one must sin every day! It would be difficult to say how great the harm is which has been done by this mistake. It is one of the chief causes why the sin of disobedience is so little recognized. I have myself heard Christians, speaking about the cause of darkness and weakness, half-laughingly, say, "Yes, it is just disobedience again." We try to get rid of a servant as speedily as possible who is habitually disobedient, but it is not regarded as anything extraordinary that a child of God should be disobedient every day. Disobedience is daily acknowledged, and yet there is no turning away from it.

Have we not here the reason why so much prayer for the power of the Holy Spirit is offered, and yet so few answers come? Do we not read that "God has given His Holy Spirit to them that obey Him"? Every child of God has received the Holy Spirit. If he uses the measure of the Holy Spirit which he has, with the definite purpose of being obedient to the utmost, then God can and will favor him with further manifestations of the Spirit's power. *Andrew Murray*

CHAPTER FOURTEEN

HE HAS PROMISED
TO ANSWER

Why does God answer prayer? I imagine that the first reason is so that He may keep His word. The simple fact about prayer is that God has agreed to answer it.

● "Ask, and it shall be given you; seek, and ye shall find; knock, and it shall be opened unto you."

● "Whatsoever ye shall ask in My name, that will I do."

● "Whatsoever ye shall ask of the Father in My name, He will give it to you."

Now, what self-respecting person speaking thus to another, and having abundant resources, would fail to do the thing that he had promised?

Sometimes we humans do fail to keep our promises, not because we are careless respecting them, but because we are unable to make them good. If God should grow wearied, or His eyes should become dim, or His abilities should in any way fail, then His promises might fail. But that His promises should fail while His wisdom and strength remain is simply impossible.

What, then, is the attitude which a person occupies respecting our heavenly Father when he talks about unanswered prayer? If this expression means anything substantial, it means that actual prayer is offered. By actual prayer I mean prayer that meets the conditions on which God has agreed to answer. Nothing else is prayer. No one has a right to call anything else prayer. This expression, then, means that prayer, actual prayer, is offered and that God breaks His word. If these people would put in some time limitation, if they would say, "for a time," or use some equivalent expression, it would be better. But to say "unanswered prayer," when God's word is pledged and all the resources of heaven are involved in the promise, seems to me an awful thing to do.

Settle Back on God's Truthfulness

This is a scriptural expression, "God that cannot lie." God's character is such that He never will wish to deceive, so He describes Himself here as a person incapable of falsehood—God that cannot lie.

I have never tried to count the promises in the Bible. Someone who professes to have done so says there are more than 30,000. Among these exceeding great and precious promises, there is probably no one more frequently repeated than the promise to hear and answer prayer. The expression, "A prayer-hearing and a prayer-answering God," is one of the most common among Christian people in their gatherings for worship.

When we meet to speak together of God's relation to our needs, it is natural that we should think of Him as one who hears and answers prayer.

● "Call unto Me, and I will answer thee, and show thee great and mighty things, which thou knowest not" (Jer. 33:3).

● "Fear thou not, for I am with thee; be not dismayed, for I am thy God; I will strengthen thee; yea, I will help thee; yea, I will uphold thee with the right hand of My righteousness" (Isa. 41:10).

God's Excellent Medicine

In an age or land where the Bible is neglected, all sorts of evils prevail. I knew of a physician who was visited by a lady who said to him, "Doctor, I do not know what the trouble is, but I am in misery. Please find out what the matter is and give me something."

He looked at her steadily for a moment and said, "You go home and read the Bible an hour every day for thirty days.

Then come and see me."

"I suppose you think I am a heathen."

"No, I do not think you are a heathen. I think you are a poor, sick, tired woman. You go home and read the Bible an hour a day for thirty days, and then come and see me."

At first indignant and resolved that she would pay no attention to his prescription, her better mind came as she went along and she said to herself, "The medicine is cheap. I will try it." Arriving at her home, she arranged matters and settled down to read. She knew that an hour was longer than she had generally read the Bible at one time, so she read longer than usual. She glanced up at the clock at the expiration of what she felt sure was an hour, and found that she had been reading just ten minutes. This startled her, for she was at heart a good woman, and she said to herself, "I will not make that mistake again. I will be sure to read an hour before I stop." So she glanced at the clock and started again.

When she felt sure that she had read for more than an hour, she glanced again at the clock and found that she had been reading twenty-five mintues. This waked her thoroughly and, adjusting herself to the task, she read until, instead of being a little weary and wishing to stop, she obtained an appetite for the Word of God. The hour was all too short and she found herself living in a new world.

At the end of the month she reported to her physician. As soon as she came into the office, he said to her, "Well, madam, I see you have been taking my medicine."

"Yes, I have been taking your medicine and it is good medicine. I am a different woman from the one who came into your office a month ago."

"Yes, I saw as soon as you came into the room that what you needed was not medicine nor anything else that man could give or do. What you needed was God. You have come in touch with Him. Keep in touch with Him and you will be well."

I have a friend in Chicago, a praying physician who is very successful in his work. One of his patients not long ago said to a friend, "I went in to see Dr. Brown the other day, and what do you think he did? He said to me, 'I wish to read to you a chapter out of the Bible,' and he actually opened the Bible, sat there and read to me a long chapter of the Book. It did me a lot of good too. It was very wonderful how it affected me. I think it was better than any of his medicine."

It is the essence of truth to harmonize with all other truth and it is the essence of error to harmonize with nothing, not even with other error. The trouble with most people is that they are ignorant of the truth. Neglecting or refusing to live in truth, they are overwhelmed in the multitude of contradictions and cannot agree among themselves. This is the explanation of the murders, suicides, the insanities which make up so large a portion of our daily news. If we could settle back on the truthfulness of God, could for ourselves aspire also to this truthfulness, could read both His promises and His threatenings with unquestioning faith, sure that He will do exactly what He has said He will do, we should then be in a fair way to get on. We should avoid evil; we should follow righteousness. We should have great comfort and gladness in our lives. We should be helpful to other people, and day by day we should grow in grace and in the knowledge of God.

Let us once more recall the fact that God answers prayer because He has promised to answer prayer, and that the heavens and the earth will pass away before one of the words which He has spoken will fail.

It is true that Bible prayers in word and print are short, but the praying men of the Bible were with God through many a sweet and holy wrestling hour. They won by few words but long waiting. The prayers Moses records may be short, but Moses prayed to God with fastings and mighty cryings forty days and nights.

The statement of Elijah's praying may be condensed to a few brief paragraphs, but doubtless Elijah, who when "praying he prayed," spent many hours of fiery struggle and lofty intercourse with God before he could, with assured boldness, say to Ahab, "There shall not be dew nor rain these years, but according to my word." The verbal brief of Paul's prayers is short, but Paul "prayed night and day exceedingly." The Lord's Prayer is a divine epitome for infant lips, but the Man Christ Jesus prayed many an all-night ere His work was done; and His all-night and long-sustained devotions gave to His work its finish and perfection, and to His character the fullness and glory of its divinity.

Spiritual work is taxing work, and men are loath to do it. Praying, true praying, costs an outlay of serious attention and of time, which flesh and blood do not relish. Few persons are made of such strong fiber that they will make a costly outlay when surface work will pass as well in the market.   E.M. *Bounds*

CHAPTER FIFTEEN

HE LOVES HIS OWN

It is one of the tragedies of human life that sometimes God seems to give a great and consuming love to one human heart for another human heart which cannot respond. Some people doubt that there is such a thing as dying of a broken heart. Yet I think there are many such cases, true and loyal hearts longing for a response that never comes.

I read of a man who was riding to the city with his nephew. The nephew said to his uncle, "I am going to buy a few presents for my wife and for my mother."

The uncle said, "I never did much of that. I used to buy candy once in a while for the children but that was all."

The nephew replied: "Try it, Uncle. Make Aunty a New Year's present and see how it will work."

The elder man dropped into a quiet mood and did not talk a great deal as they finished their journey. Later the younger man, having completed his errand and going into a large dry-goods store to gather up an armful of bundles, found his uncle fingering a soft gray silk. After the nephew had aided the uncle in selecting the dress pattern, the uncle confided to him in a bashful sort of way that he had also bought her a silver mounted toilet set—brush and comb and glass—and some other little things, and said, "I am almost scared to give them to her."

"Well, Uncle," said the boy, "they won't hurt her any. You tell me how it worked when you get through."

After the Christmas had come, the nephew called upon his aunt and uncle and the uncle seemed more than ever embarrassed and hesitant. Finally, when they were alone, he said, "I put them on the bed and went out of the room so that she might find them. She did not come out and I got scared for fear that something had happened. When I went and looked through the door, she was on her knees by the bed, sobbing over my gifts, and when I came into the room she came to me and called me 'Pa' and kissed me." It is unfortunate and not an uncommon thing tht good people who really love one another should live thus without the expression of affection until it is too late—flowers on the coffin so many times where there are no flowers in the life time.

We Are Dear to God

There is no person, young or old, who is not dear to the heart of God. Even if you are living in sin, still you are dear to the heart of God. Jesus Christ left His throne in heaven and came to this world to live the humble, self-denying life that He lived, and die a shameful, agonizing death on the cross, and lie in a cave in the world which He Himself made, because He loves you. He is the changeless One. He loves men now as well as He did 2,000 years ago and He will love them 2,000 years hence as truly and with as God-like fervor as He loves them now. It is one of the character-istics of affection that it seeks to supply needed good and seeks to ward off threatening evil from the loved being. This is an explanation of the fact that God makes so many promises to prayer and keeps them all.

My youngest girl was born happy. I remember when she was four or five years of age that she would run from one end of a long room to the other, stop a moment, jump up and down four or five times and say, "Oh, I am so happy! Oh, I am so happy!" My impression is that this sort of gladness is found more frequently among young children than among persons who are older. Even when men and women are as glad as she, the realities of life give them a more sober tone. This is natural and we would not wish it to be otherwise. Yet beyond question, it is the will of God that every one of His children should be glad.

The sadness, the tears, the cries of pain that occasionally

shock our own ears sadden also the heart of God. When He sees His children happy and glad, I know that He is pleased. When He finds them grieved and sad, I am sure He desires to administer the help which will make them as pleased as He would gladly see them.

He Cares for Physical Needs

Our bodies are of the earth and time. Someone has said, "When we begin to live, we begin to die." This is not exactly true, but there is truth in it.

A friend who is an intern in a hospital said to me, "In our hospital men, women and little children are dying every day, and it is pitiful to see in how many ways death comes upon them." My own daughter was night superintendent at a great hospital and I one time said to her, "How do people feel when they come to the hospitals?" "O Papa," she replied, "before they come to the hospital they have suffered so long and suffered so much that they do not think much of anything. They are a bit afraid but they hope that some way or other they may be helped." One of the things which drives people to prayer is physical need. Aches and pains, wasting, multilation, impending death— these are the things which drive them to God and God sympathizes with these sufferings and seeks to relieve them so far as possible without spiritual injury to those who pray.

God has placed in the world remedies which naturally counteract every disease under which men suffer. He has given men skill to ascertain these remedies and to use them for the relief of suffering. In tens of thousands of instances where human skill was unavailing, or where natural remedies failed, He has directly entered into the physical lives of men to rebuke diseases, to rebuke diseases of the most serious sort and to heal those who were sick.

The healing of bodily ailments was one of the most common things in the life of Jesus. It is not recorded that in any one instance Jesus said that the disease was so serious or of such long continuance that it had passed beyond His power. In no single instance did Jesus disregard a prayer for physical healing which the suffering ones uttered unto His ear. If He is the same yesterday, today and forever, why should He not answer the prayer of the rheumatic, the fever-smitten, the consumptive, the paralytic who come to Him, driven by their needs? There is no doubt but that He is doing this sort of thing continually, and He says to physical sufferers now, just as He did in the olden days, "Ask, and ye shall receive, that your joy may be full" (John 16:24).

He Cares for Spiritual Afflictions

It is possible to attach too much importance to the healing of the body, for it is more important that the spirit be well and strong. "The spirit of a man will sustain his infirmity; but a wounded spirit who can bear?" (Prov. 18:14) That is, it is better to have a weak body with a strong spirit than to have a weak and wounded spirit, even though the body be well.

Spiritual suffering is caused at times by temptations. How fiercely the fire burns against the soul! Temptations of the flesh, temptations of the world, temptations direct from Satan, the ruler of hell—these temptations are so real oftentimes, so long continued, that the soul suffers. As the Word says, "Ye are in heaviness through manifold temptations" (1 Peter 1:6). It is in such times that we experience what the psalmist did when he said, "My soul cleaveth unto the dust; quicken Thou me according to Thy word" (Ps. 119:25). Wise men in such times pray and God hears their prayers. Sometimes He helps them one way, sometimes another; but He always hears and helps them if they really pray.

A poor fellow who was overloaded cried out, "Lord, lighten my burden, or strengthen my back." It was a wise prayer, for God sometimes increases our strength and sometimes lightens our load. If in times of great physical affliction or times of great temptation a person gives way to petulance, to anger, to irritability, and murmurs and complains against God, he increases his difficulty and deprives himself of vast remedies; for God does not permit any evil to come upon men without the hope of doing them good. How oftentimes His father heart is grieved because He cannot help us as He would.

He Cares for Financial Difficulties

Another prolific source of human sorrows is financial stress. While we live in these human bodies, we shall need food, clothing and shelter. They may be very primitive or they may be more elaborate, but they are always needful. Sometimes by our own fault, sometimes by the fault of others, sometimes apparently without anyone's fault, there is dire need and distress because of the need. I think perhaps quite as common as suffering from physical ailment or temptation or spiritual difficulty, is suffering from the lack of money and the things which money can procure.

Oftentimes those who suffer are proud and suffer in silence. Many times they are not willing to have their need known. Sometimes they are not willing to have it supplied. But when hunger or cold grind and bite, their pride is very apt to give way. Even if they cannot consent to speak to their fellowmen, oftentimes there is a cry in their hearts after God. The ways in which God answers these prayers for help are numberless—sometimes through the hands and hearts of others, sometimes through increased wisdom and strength on the part of the needy one, sometimes by providential changes in the channels of trade, sometimes by what the world calls mere accidents. In one way or another, God meets the needs of men.

I read of a merchant who was caught with a large amount of paper in the banks at a time when making loans was nearly impossible. He went to the banks with which he had extensive dealings and without exception the officers said to him that they were withdrawing credits, not extending them, and that they could not let him have a dollar.

Heavyhearted, he went to his home and his wife, meeting him at the door, said to him, "Why, Husband, are you sick?"

"No," he said, "I am not sick, but we are ruined."

"What is the matter?" she asked, and he related the facts as I have stated them before.

She smiled when he had completed his story and said to him, "Is that all?"

"All? I should think that was enough. This house will have to be sold. You will have to live in a rented house or in a cottage. Tomorrow I shall be posted throughout the city as a bankrupt. I should think that was enough."

"Have you prayed?"

"No, I had not thought of that yet."

"Why, that is the first thing to do. Let us pray together and then trust God and all will be well."

They went to prayer. God heard them and then they went to sleep.

In the morning he went early to his office but had hardly entered it before the president of one of the banks of the city came in and said to him, "You were, I believe, in the bank yesterday afternoon."

"Yes," he said, "I needed some money for paper falling due today and I was in your bank."

"I believe the cashier told you you could not draw on us at this time."

"Yes," the merchant replied, "that is what he said."

"Well, we have conferred about the matter and we have decided that you may draw on us up to $50,000." It was quite sufficient to carry him over the strain and he came through the time of an actual panic without impairment of credit.

There is no doubt at all but that thousands of men who fail would experience the same mercy if they would ask in the same way.

Not long since I read of two men in a small town, one of whom knew how to pray, the other of whom did not. They went to their homes heavyhearted. The one who knew how to pray did so, and courage and help came to him. He went through the time without loss of honor and without serious losses of other kinds. The man who did not know how to pray went into his bathroom and shot himself. His wife and children gathered up the poor body and buried it, but they could never bury the memory.

It pays to pray. The silver and the gold are God's, "and the cattle upon a thousand hills" (Ps. 50:10). "The earth is the Lord's, and the fullness thereof; the world, and they that dwell therein" (Ps. 24:1). Your heavenly Father knoweth what things you have need of. "Ask, and ye shall receive, that your joy may be full."

He Cares About Trouble With People

Sometimes we are troubled by other human beings. Children do not do right. Parents do not do right. Husbands grieve wives, wives grieve husbands. Neighbors are not kind to neighbors. At times these difficulties with humans are trifling. They are what we call vexations. At other times thay rise to fearful heights and fairly swamp the soul. Whether they be more or less serious, the remedy is the same. In fact, if they are dealt with promptly at the beginning, they are not likely to become so serious as if they are neglected. "The king's heart is in the hand of the Lord, as the rivers of water; He turneth it withersoever He will" (Prov. 21:1).

I have over and over again, in my home life, in my school life, in my church life, in my community life, experienced the truth that God is able to save us from these difficulties with humans. I am not saying that all people are equally agreeable. Everyone knows that it would not be true. Yet it is possible to live in a measure of peace and harmony with most individuals. We do not have to quarrel and we are not required ordinarily to suffer greatly in our relations with our fellow beings. If we are humble, if pride and self-will can be definitely nailed to the cross of Jesus Christ, there will not be many times in our lives when we cannot be fairly comfortable with the people about us.

But if we murmur and complain when we ought to pray, difficulties will continue and increase. Difficulties which in the beginning are trials light as air may grow to such dimensions that they will destroy the peace of churches, communities, that they will alienate hearts forever. There is a blessing pronounced upon peacemakers and we all should aspire to this blessing. If we cannot ourselves attain to the blessing of the peacemaker, we ought at least to attain to the blessing of the peacekeeper. If we cannot harmonize and unite those who are at enmity, we should be able to avoid worrying and distressing other folk. It is very sad to see good people who are continually at variance with their fellows.

A man who was in many respects one of the best men I ever knew—pure in his life, genial in his relations with those who were next to him, absolutely honest in his purposes and intentions—was everlastingly in quarrel and litigation with somebody. I never knew a more tireless laborer in my life. He nearly killed himself with his work, but he died in comparative poverty after having lost two fortunes, when it was entirely within his power to have fallen asleep in Jesus, universally regretted, and with all the comforts of life about him. I think of him often when this subject comes up, for I do not think he prayed enough. I know he did not pray enough with the people of God. He worked so diligently with his hands that it was hard for him to go to prayer meetings at all. Ordinarily, he was not in the weekly church prayer meeting and this was one of the things that marred his peace and crippled his influence for good.

God answers prayer because He loves His children. He would answer more prayer if there was more prayer for Him to answer. He does not wish one person to be long troubled in body or spirit or in social relations. A rest remains for the people of God. "Thou wilt keep him in perfect peace, whose mind is stayed on Thee: because he trusteth in Thee" (Isa. 26:3). The trusting spirit prays to learn and learns to pray, and receives things from God. So, brethren, let us be careful about prayer.

This faith sheds a wholly new light on the life of obedience. Christ holds Himself responsible to work in me every moment, if I only trust Him for it. Then I begin to understand the important phrase with which Paul begins and closes his Epistle to the Romans (Rom. 1:5; 16:26): "The obedience of faith." Faith brings me to the Lord Jesus, not only to obtain the forgiveness of sin, but also that I may every moment enjoy the power which will make it possible for me, as a child of God, to abide in Him, and to be numbered among His obedient children—of whom it is written that, as He who has called them is holy, so they also may be holy in all manner of conversation. Everything depends on whether or not I believe on the whole Christ, with the fullness of His grace, that He will (not now and then but) every moment be the strength of my life. Such faith will lead to an obedience which will enable me to "walk worthy of the Lord unto all pleasing, being fruitful in every good work, strengthened with all might, according to His glorious power."

The soul which feeds on such promises will experience now, instead of the disobedience of self-effort, what the obedience of faith means. All such promises have their measure, their certainty, and their strength in the living Christ. *Andrew Murray*

CHAPTER SIXTEEN

HE WISHES US
TO SERVE OTHERS

Some people believe that the chief duty of Christians is to attain to happiness. Jesus said, "These things have I spoken unto you, that My joy might remain in you, and that your joy might be full" (John 15:11).

If we were to put the desire of God for us into a single sentence, perhaps we could not speak more truthfully than to say that He wishes us to be glad. Yet there is no such thing as a selfish gladness which shall be permanent. Selfishness is a deadly poison and, if permitted in the heart of any person, will work out bitterness and death. If we are truly glad, other people will share in our sunshine. This is inevitable, and part of the divine plan. God answers our prayers, because He wishes us to help our fellows.

The Contagion of Example

The mere fact that God has answered our prayers will encourage other people to pray and to secure good things from God if they find out what He has done for us in answer to petition. I heard a man, who had been so ruined by sin that life seemed to hold nothing more for him, say that in his helplessness and despair he stumbled into a meeting of the Salvation Army. Dazed and crushed, he listened to man after man telling what God had done for them. Finally, leaving the room and going to the miserable abode which he called home, he fell upon his knees and said, "O Lord, You helped those other fellows, please help me." He said that from that hour he was delivered—that God did exactly the thing he asked Him to do, helped him in the way He helped the others.

Several years ago I wrote in *The Christian Endeavor World* that I was at one time unable to get into my office. Various keys had been used and the bolt had passed out of position so that the key that should have struck against the notch, struck against the smooth edge of the bar. At the time, I did not know what the matter was. I only knew that my guest wished his suitcase and I could not get it for him. After having tried several moments and having others do the same unavailingly, I said to one of the janitors, "Will you kindly see that this door is opened? We shall need to get this gentleman's suitcase for the train at 3 o'clock."

He consented to do so and we went on to our luncheon. Returning at 3 o'clock, in scant time for the train, I found the lock in exactly the condition it had been. I turned the key forward and backward, and did not know what to do. At last it occurred to me that I had not prayed, so as I stood by the door I said, "Lord, You know that this gentleman needs his baggage and I cannot get it for him in time for the train unless You help. Please make this key throw this bolt." Having thus prayed, I turned the key. As if there had never been the slightest difficulty, the bolt shot back and the door was open!

I mentioned this to two brother ministers at my table that day or the next, and one of them said, "I never would bother the Lord about a little thing like that. I would consult a locksmith." So would I have consulted a locksmith had there been time; but if I had waited to do so, my friend could not have had his suitcase in time for his train. I was glad that God gave it to him.

Not long afterward one of my neighbors mentioned that she had read about this in *The Christian Endeavor World*. She said that her stove had been out of order for some weeks, that she had asked the stove man to come and put it in order, that he had failed to do so, and that her husband had repeatedly gone to the city with the memory of a smoky kitchen and a poor breakfast. Having read this article, she said to herself, "If God in answer to prayer will help unlock a door, why would He not help me with my stove, to get my husband a decent breakfast?" So she prayed that God would help her about the stove. She told me, "I do not pretend to know what the reason was for the change. The only difference that I know about was that I had prayed." Whatever may have been the explanation, the stove drew perfectly from the beginning and her husband had a hot breakfast and a clean house to remember as he went away to the train.

In our Christian lives, from beginning to end, there is nothing more commonplace than the force of example. God helps one person to do a thing, and somebody else, learning of this assistance, asks for and receives the same. This is true everywhere and is one reason, no doubt, why God answers our prayers, in order that we may assist other people by telling them of the answers which we have received, and thus encouraging them to ask and receive so that their joy also may be full.

The Desire To Serve

When we have prayed and have received the joy of the Lord in our lives as a result, we are in a condition to be helpful to other people by our own activities. One of the reasons why we do not help others more is that we do not care to. Of course this is failure. I shall not do any more good than I wish to.

But another reason why we oftentimes fail in helping our fellows is that we do not know how or we have not the power. This knowledge and this power are gained by prayer and if we thus pray, God answers our prayers that we may be helpful to our fellows. I think most of our readers will have at some time heard the gospel song, "Make Me a Channel of Blessing Today." The sentiment is perfectly Christian and an explanation of the great usefulness of certain persons. God wishes to make us blessings; and if we ask for knowledge as to method, or for power to carry out a proposed form, He is certain to help us.

I was riding into Boston one morning. I sat in the coach praying as we were coming into the station, and my prayer was that the Lord would enable me to be of service to some of His children that day. When I stepped on the platform I saw immediately before me a little Italian woman. She had a baby in her arms, a child perhaps three years of age, hanging on to her skirts, a satchel in the free hand and a large bundle of clothes lying on the platform. She looked very helpless and instantly the Spirit said to me, "Here they are."

So I took the bundle of clothes and the grip. She looked at me closely for a moment, but evidently made up her mind that I did not intend to do any harm. I said to her in very good English, which she did not understand though she could perfectly understand my look and act, "Come on, let us go down." So we went the long length of that platform in the South Station to the concourse, where I found directly the interpreter who took care of the Italian immigrants. He took her baggage, spoke to her in her native tongue and put her in the way where she wished to go. It was a very little thing to do, but it was an answer to prayer and it helped me to be helpful.

One day as I was on my way to take a train from Wheaton to Chicago for a meeting, I met an unfortunate lady who reported that she had been robbed of practically all her money, that she had been ordered out of her boardinghouse, and that she did not know which way to turn or what to do. I was as perplexed as she. When we got on to the train, I looked through the train to find a seat for her and finally, in the far back of the coach, found a single empty seat, no other empty seat being near it. I then went forward through the car, looking for a place for myself. I finally found two seats facing one another, in which there was an old lady and two children.

I sat down in the vacant seat, facing the old lady. I did not know her, but after a moment she said to me, "I think you are President Blanchard."

I said, "Yes, my name is Blanchard. May I know to whom I am speaking?"

She gave me her name and said to me, "I have been in city mission work in Chicago for many years and I have frequently heard you preach in the Moody Church."

I asked her, "If you were to meet a lady tonight who had no money, who had been ordered out of her boardinghouse because she was already in arrears and could not pay, is there any place in Chicago where you could take such a person where she would be safe and comfortable?"

"Oh, yes," she said, and named a home.

"I have a friend here on the train who is in that condition. Would you be willing to meet her?"

"Certainly, I should be glad." So I went back to the place where this lady was sitting and brought her forward and put her down in the seat where I had been, introducing her to this city missionary lady. The latter was some distance from home and had quite a journey to make to the north of the city, but she postponed her departure and went with this needy sister to the south side and housed her safely.

I did not hear the result of the transaction until two or three years later when I met the missionary again. She mentioned the occurrence and said that she was glad to say that that lady was kept safely in this home until her skies lightened and she was able to accomplish the thing that she desired. God helps us that we may help others. There is no doubt about it.

The Need of Testimony

I fear because I mention at times little things that God has permitted me to do for others, that I shall create the impression that I have always been faithful and successful in such matters. This is not at all true. My failures have been far more than my successful services, but I do not see that it would glorify God for me to speak of the times when by forgetfulness, by inattention, by self-neglect, I have failed to accomplish what God has put within my power. Because I am trying to encourage people to pray for their own comfort, for the help of other people, I mention the instances in my own life and in the lives of others which I think will put them about the work which they ought to do.

Among all the millions of people who live in this world, so few are carefree, so many are burdened. God has in His heart not some of these people but every one of them and He has at His command—in the way of physical well-being, spiritual help, material resources—all and more than all that they require. Yet there are these tens of millions, hundreds of millions, many of them in Christian lands, who do not know how to go to Him for the things which they need. How are they to learn unless some of those who have found the road, point it out to those who are yet in ignorance of it?

This calls up another question which is related. I speak of the duty of testimony concerning the answers to our prayers. To pray is one thing. Believing for answers is a second part of all real prayer. Testimony to these answers is a third thing, which differs from the first two;, and an answer which is not recorded will die with those immediately concerned, while an answer which is mentioned to the praise of God will become a fountain, sending its sweet waters far and wide through the desert lands in which human hearts are suffering.

I mention here two narratives of fact which impressed me deeply, which I have already reported to the people of God through *The Christian Endeavor World,* but which I mention here for the encouragement of God's people. I am sure that the facts are as stated, for I knew the people well. They have lived near me for years and I am certain that those who will believe and ask may also receive and thus their joy may become full.

● A student's faith tested. When a well-known Christian teacher was a young student, he was studying in a school where meals were served only for cash, and where payments were made by the meal. One night he was in a mission, and among the friends present was a poor woman with a little child. He had at the time only seventy-five cents, but felt strongly moved by the suffering of the woman and the child, so that in the end he gave them all that he had, walking home through the streets with an empty pocket but a glad heart.

He thought, inasmuch as he had given all his money to one of God's suffering ones, God would in some way provide him with a breakfast the next morning. The morning came, and the breakfast for others; but there was nothing for him. He was a strong young man with a good appetite arising from plenty of hard work. He said, "This is all right; no doubt something will come by dinnertime." He thought that he should find the money on the sidewalk, or that a friend would hand it to him, or that he would get some payment for work, or that in some way God would provide him with a dinner. But He did not, and there was no dinner for him. It was so at suppertime, and so the next morning.

By this time he was ravenously hungry. It was suggested to his mind that there were scores of fellows around him who would lend him what he needed and that he could repay them. But he said, "No, I will not borrow money. I expect to be a preacher, and to tell people that if they do right, God will take care of them. I will see this thing through; and if God does not take care of me, I will never preach to other people that God will take care of them."

There was no dinner that second day, nor supper, nor breakfast the third morning; and still he believed in God, and waited His time. Toward the middle of the forenoon one of the instructors of the institution called him aside, and said, "I have received this check with direction to give it to someone who will use it wisely; and I have decided to give it to you." It was a check for $36. He cashed it, and provided for his bodily needs in the way of food, and then had sufficient left to secure clothing, which he was also needing. From that time to this present he has never passed through such a testing time as God gave him on that occasion.

● The poorhouse in prospect. A lady said to me that shortly after her marriage, the father and mother of her husband were in serious financial difficulties. A mortgage threatened to eat up their home, and they did not have money for daily needs, even if the house had been free.

Her mother-in-law said to her, "Father and I must go to the poorhouse; there is nothing else left for us to do." She replied, "Never, while I am alive."

After she and her husband had looked over the situation, they agreed to move to the home of the father and mother and to join their slender earnings with those of the parents to secure the home and to keep the daily needs supplied.

Some years after this resolution had been put into execution, her husband lost his situation and failed to secure anything else. In this extremity he opened a small place, and began a business for himself; but it seemed that all the business went in other directions. For weeks, the income of the family amounted to not more than fifty cents per week. These saints first paid their tithe, and then lived on the remainder, absolutely refusing to go into debt even for a loaf of bread. She said to me, "There were many days when for myself and for each one of the children I put down half a piece of bread, gave thanks to God, and knew that He would deliver us in due time."

One morning she did not have the half piece of bread in the household. There was absolutely nothing except a little flour, and she had nothing with which to cook that except water. In this extremity she went to her room and laid the matter before God. She said to Him, "You know we are Your children, seeking to do Your will; that we have not robbed You in tithes and offerings. You know how hard it is for me to see the children hungry, and how my own strength is weakened for lack of food; and You know that I rely upon You to supply our need."

After a few moments a neighbor who had no knowledge of the situation came into the house and said to her, "We have a Jersey cow, and we cannot use all the milk; and I also have a pint of cream which is sour, but which I should be glad if you could use."

She thanked her, went into the next room, where her father-in-law and mother-in-law lived, and said, "See what God has sent us. I have flour; now, if you will let me have a little lard and baking soda, we can have some hot biscuits."

She was about preparing them when another neighbor came in, also ignorant of the situation, and said to her, "I have just received a box from my home on the farm. There are more things in it than we know how to use, and I have taken the liberty of bringing some over to you." She proceeded to lay down on the table a quantity of sweet potatoes, a supply of bacon and ham, and other provisions of like sort, until the table was almost covered.

Pretty soon a third neighbor, whose husband kept a

small grocery store nearby, came in and said to her, "I do not want you to be offended, but I have here about six pounds of butter which is a little too óld for table use, but which is good for cooking; and I should be glad to leave it with you, if you can use it. I have a gallon of honey drips. My children like honey drips, and I think yours will too. I also have a little canned fruit which has been standing on our shelves, and which ought to be used up. So I took the liberty to bring that over also. If you are willing, I should be glad to leave these all for you."

"Well," said this dear friend, "we had a great table, the hot biscuits, and the sweet potatoes, and the honey drips, and the other gifts which we had not known for weeks and months."

Let the redeemed of the Lord say that they are redeemed!

The Holy Spirit is "the Spirit of prayer." He is definitely called by this name in Zechariah 12:10: "The Spirit of grace and of supplications." Twice in Paul's epistles there is a remarkable reference to Him in the matter of prayer. "Ye have received the Spirit of adoption, whereby we cry, 'Abba, Father' " (Rom. 8:15). "God hath sent forth the Spirit of His Son into your hearts, crying, 'Abba, Father' " (Gal. 4:6). Have you ever meditated on these words: "Abba, Father"? In that name our Saviour offered His greatest prayer to the Father, accompanied by the entire surrender and sacrifice of His life and love. The Holy Spirit is given for the express purpose of teaching us, from the very beginning of our Christian life onward, to utter that word in childlike trust and surrender. In one of these passages we read: "We cry;" in the other: "He cries." What a wonderful blending of the divine and human cooperation in prayer. What a proof that God—if I may say so—has done His utmost to make prayer as natural and effectual as though it were the cry of a child to an earthly father, as he says, "Abba, Father."

Is it not a proof that the Holy Spirit is to a great extent a stranger in the church, when prayer, for which God has made such provision, is regarded as a task and a burden? And does not this teach us to seek for the deep root of prayerlessness in our ignorance of, and disobedience to, the Divine Instructor whom the Father has commissioned to teach us to pray? *Andrew Murray*

CHAPTER SEVENTEEN

WE TAP THE
INFINITE RESERVOIRS

I t is one of the un-
pleasant facts connected with present educational life in the
United States that presidents of colleges are required to
spend so much of their time in serving tables; that is to say,
the raising of funds and the expenditure of funds require a
large portion of the thought and time of the college
president.

The man who ought to be continually occupied with the
soul-life of his students, who should have time to think and
pray and labor for the spiritual uplift of those who are to be
centers of life and power in the coming age, seems con-
demned to spend much of his time on questions relating to
endowments, buildings, libraries, and so forth.

Some years ago I began to ask our heavenly Father that
He would lessen my labors in that direction and set me
more at liberty for the intellectual and spiritual labors which
are the proper office of a college man.

Three Definite Requests

I made three petitions. The first was that if it were the
divine will, friends who were contributing regularly to the
funds of Wheaton College might be led to bestow larger
sums than they had been hitherto giving. This was not
intended to be an added tax on them, but an enlarged proportion out of the funds devoted to a work which is fundamental and far-reaching in character.

This petition was almost immediately granted. Without solicitation, people who had been giving certain sums annually or occasionally began to double, in some instances to quadruple, their gifts. The result was that the time required for securing the needed money was greatly reduced, and the effort required was also lessened.

The second request was that God would incline persons who had not been requested to contribute to college needs, persons of whom we did not know, to make appropriations for the work. This was desired as à testimony to the promise-keeping, prayer-hearing character of our Heavenly Father.

Though all good gifts are from Him, whether they are requested or not, the gift which is bestowed without any human intervention seems more obviously His work than that which comes in answer to any solicitation. In the one case there is the impress of the divine Spirit alone; in the other case there is the divine action through the human instrumentality. Both are divine, but this characteristic is more evident in the case where the human is not in any measure involved.

The third petition was that a human helper might be bestowed, if it were the divine will, so that the cares and labors of this sort which were necessary might be divided, so that my own hands might be set more at liberty for what is undoubtedly the principal duty of one who has the care of souls.

Later, when I was at a large meeting in the city of Chicago, a gentleman of whom I had never heard approached me and asked for a place in the college life such as I had prayed for.

After inquiry had been made from those to whom he referred, he was engaged for service in this direction, and with human limitations proved to be a God-ordained helper.

My second request was a plea for the special honor of our Heavenly Father, a request that He would directly move on the hearts of people irrespective of any human agency.

Shortly after I began to make this request of God, a gentleman in Chicago who was an old and valued friend, and who had at various times contributed small sums to the work of the College, passed away. He had spent his life in the ministry, and had no considerable property; but out of the estate which he had he directed his executors to pay to the College the sum of $100. Under some circumstances this would not have been an impressive fact, but under the circumstances which then existed it seemed a very impressive fact. It seemed to be the first item in what I believed would be a long answer to a large request.

Not long after, I received word that an old friend had died. It had been thirty or forty years since I had been intimately associated with him. He was at that time a minister, and was serving poor congregations in one of the smallest of our church organizations. When his children came to college, they were closely limited in their expenditures. I had never known of any change in his circumstances, and had never requested any gifts from him for any department of college work. I think I should have more naturally thought of offering him some small token of brotherly regard than of suggesting that he do anything for the College.

I was notified that he had made the College one of his heirs, and a property was by him bestowed which would have netted the college $1,000, if a few years' delay had been expedient. It was, however, sold for $600, which was needed then.

Shortly thereafter, I received word from attorneys in Iowa that the College was heir to an estate in that commonwealth. Looking the matter up, I found that a lady whom I had never seen, but to whom I had written several years before, had willed a large portion of her estate to the institution.

I had written to her only once or twice, and then without any expectation of any large gift. I had no knowledge of her resources. In fact, her close friends did not know what they were, and told me they were surprised to find them so considerable.

Her executor proved to be a Christian gentleman who expressed his readiness to pay to the College immediately the amount of her bequest less a reasonable reservation for possible bills yet to be presented.

The result of that transaction was that something more than $6,000 came to the treasury at a time when it was very greatly needed. The gift also contributed largely toward securing the endowment fund.

About two years after this transaction had been completed, I received word from a stranger is Missouri, notifying me that a relative in Kansas had made the College one of his heirs, and requesting that we look after the matter. We learned that the gentleman had left three-fourths of his property to the College and the remaining one-fourth to a local beneficence in which he was interested.

There was no reason why this gift should not have been paid over at once; but various interested persons, who desired to secure a portion of it for themselves, prevented the immediate settlement which might have been made and which would have accomplished the desire of the testator. Nevertheless, when the matter was finally concluded, the College received more than $10,000 from that estate, $6,000 of which was passed to the endowment account, the remainder being used for current expenses.

In 1913 we received word from New Hampshire that a lady there, also a stranger to us, had directed the executor of her estate to pay to the College the sum of $3,000. With this sum, less the inheritance tax, we have record of more than $20,000 which has been provided for the work of Wheaton College without any intervention by agencies or requests.

Two Methods

To me this is very significant, indicating the power and disposition of God to provide for the needs of the College by direct impulse on the minds and hearts of men and women, rather than through the solicitation of others.

Why then should we not discontinue agencies? I think this question is inevitable, and it naturally rises in the minds of thoughtful people. If God is able, and if He is disposed to provide for His work and the needs of His church without human effort, why should we not discontinue all effort, making our petitions to Him and to Him alone? For some of God's children, this is undoubtedly the method they should pursue.

There have been in various parts of the world great enterprises which have been carried forward in the same manner, that is, by direct petition to God without the employment of any human instrumentalities. *The Life of Trust*, by George Müller, seems to be decisive in regard to this subject.

It is my impression that this method of carrying on the Lord's work is in important respects more honorable to our heavenly Father, more stimulating to faith, and more an occasion of gratitude and thanksgiving than other methods which the Lord's people sometimes seem directed to use.

A valued friend, having learned to receive things from God in answer to prayer, said to me, "My motto is, 'Trust God, and tell His people.' " While I am still of the opinion that the former method is the ideal, and should be employed whenever one is so directed, I am of the opinion that this second method may sometimes be the divine plan for God's people. There are a number of reasons for this opinion.

In the first place, there is the resulting communion of saints, both in the imparting of information and in the sharing of God's material gifts.

In the Jewish system there was a careful provision for the meeting and communion of God's chosen ones. Three times in the year the adult Israelites had their great gatherings. They spent days together, entirely free from ordinary occupations. There was time for what we should call visiting, which is in itself a means of grace, and which is sadly neglected in our own time. If those who represent God's work are consecrated men and women, the necessary meeting with other people individually and in assemblies is of itself a means of grace.

There is also the truth indicated by the proverb, "Information is inspiration." God employs all the knowledge which His people possess as a means of inspiring them for His work. Sometimes this knowledge is communicated through the printed page as reports are sent out to earnest people who are ready to do whatever God wants, but who would not know what He wants if they did not receive the information.

At times this same information may be communicated in a personal conversation in an office or a parlor. At other times it may be imparted through public addresses; but no matter how the work is done, God's people need to be informed about His work. If they are informed, then they will be led to do things which the Spirit might never suggest to them if they lacked the knowledge which is thus acquired.

The third fact which may properly be stated is that God seems always disposed to bless labor. The fields yield their annual harvests because of divine power, but it is the will of God that human efforts should be combined with the divine energy. Men plough and plant and cultivate and gather in as a condition of harvest. All their efforts would be vain and useless without the divine blessing. On the other hand, the divine blessing would not be bestowed if through carelessness, indifference, or idleness, the effort of the human mind and heart and hand were kept back.

Variety in Unity

Variety in unity is a divine law. We are oftentimes reminded that this is the order in which the universe proceeds. The plan is one; the great purpose of God is to purge out from the good world which He made all those things which have marred and hindered.

This He is doing day by day, and will continue to do until the very rocks give up the record of the sins of men, and we have a new heaven and a new earth in which righteousness alone will dwell.

I often think of an illustration with which Dr. Joseph Parker of London closed his great address on "Manner in the Pulpit." He said,

A little gold watch was one day crossing Westminster Bridge at the time when Big Ben tolled out the hour of noon from the clocktower in the Parliament Buildings. The little watch looked up at the big clock, and said, "I do not like you; your face is too broad, your hands are too big, your voice is too coarse; I do not like you."

And the big clock said to the gold watch, "Come up here, little sister; come up here."

So the little watch toiled painfully up the stone steps, and at last stood by the big clock. Looking out over the surging millions of London, the big clock said to the watch, "Little sister, there is a man down there on Westminster Bridge who wishes to know the hour. Will you tell him, please?"

And the little watch said, "Oh I could never make him hear. My voice is so small it never could begin to carry in such a whirlwind of noise as this."

The big clock said, "Oh yes, little sister; I had forgotten; yet the man wishes to know the time, he requires to know, and you cannot tell him; but I can and will. So let us henceforth not criticize one another. You will not find fault with me nor I find fault with you; but each of us in our own place, you for your mistress and I for the great city, will teach men everywhere to redeem the time."

This beautiful illustration is of very wide application. It covers many things besides manner in the pulpit. It is of value also as we consider the possible ways of meeting the material needs of God's work.

How Should We Pray?

My father was a wonderful man of prayer. My earliest recollections are of hearing him pray at night in his study, which was next to the bedroom where my brother Willie and I slept. I have known him time and again to rise in the middle of the night and dress, or wrap himself in a quilt, and kneel and pray. These prayers were sometimes very long.

In my own prayer life, which has been differently directed, there were years when I felt distressed that I was not led to do as my father did. I sometimes thought that I ought to do so, irrespective of feelings, that I ought to pray God to make me pray as my father did.

But one day He said to me, "Do you wish to pray the way your father did, or do you wish to pray the way I want you to?"

I said, "Of course, I wish to pray the way You would have me; but it seems as though my father's prayers were more self-sacrificing and, because they were, must be more pleasing to You."

And He said to me, "I am well able to tell you how I wish you to pray. You have nothing to do except to be watchful and obedient. When I tell you to pray standing, stand and pray; and, when I tell you to rise from your bed, kneel, and pray, do that. Always do the thing I tell you to do, and you will be right in My sight."

This message released me from bondage, and I have since been joyously free in this as well as in many other matters. I record the facts above stated for the praise of my Heavenly Father and for the comfort and help of my brothers.

I am sure that we have not attained to even a small part of what God would be glad to do for us. I know that there are tens of thousands of burdened hearts, men and women troubled with temptations of the adversary, troubled by the failures and defects of other people, troubled by the lack of worldly resources, troubled by aches and pains in their bodies, troubled by failure to comprehend things which they need to know in order to carry forward their life tasks successfully.

To all of these dear children Jesus is saying now, just as He said long ago, "Ask, and it shall be given you; seek, and ye shall find; knock, and it shall be opened unto you. For everyone that asketh receiveth; and he that seeketh findeth; and to him that knocketh it shall be opened" (Matt. 7:7-8).

If you will turn to the appointed time for the fulfilling of Old Testament promise, you will read in Galatians 4:6, "Because ye are sons, God hath sent forth the Spirit of His Son into your hearts, crying, 'Abba, Father,' " Here we find God doing exactly what He promised to do; sending the blessed Holy Spirit, and sending Him as a Spirit of prayer, enabling us to say, "Our Father, who art in heaven." Notice in passing, please, that this Spirit is called the Spirit of His Son. Because we have the Spirit of His Son we are sons. Now read 1 John 3:1, and think of all this means! It is rich with blessing for those who understand. It is through the Son that "we both have access by one Spirit unto the Father" (Eph. 2:18). We can "come boldly to the throne of grace," because our Father sits upon it. It is the Spirit of Sonship that distinguishes prayer from beggary. "When the evidence of sonship grows dim, we knock feebly at mercy's door." *William W. Biederwolf*

"And I will bring the blind by a way that they knew not; I will lead them in paths that they have not known; I will make darkness light before them, and crooked things straight. These things will I do unto them, and not forsake them" (Isa. 42:16).

CHAPTER EIGHTEEN

HE KNOWS
WHAT WE NEED

T here is no part of our lives which is a matter of indifference to God. I once heard a man say that it was an insult to God to ask for a temporal blessing. If he was right, why did the Lord Jesus Christ tell us to say, "Give us this day our daily bread"? (Matt. 6:11) Evidently the man was mistaken. In his eagerness to emphasize one truth, he discredited another truth which is also important. The fact is, God made us the complex beings that we are. We have bodies as well as souls. We can suffer under a bruise or a cut as well as under a mistake or a sin. We can enjoy the fragrance of a clover field or a rose garden as truly as we can appreciate the thought of a kind action received.

It is true that the pain and the gladness differ. But they are both real. The fact that they differ proves the complexity of our being. The fact that they are real shows that God must be interested in them both.

Now, God answers prayer because He is interested in us just as we are. How pitiful, now absurd it would be if God should make us complex beings and then be interested in only one side of our existence—if God should make us so that we need bread and water, and then provide for us nothing but air and the influences of His Holy Spirit. The latter are no doubt important, but so are the former. God is interested in everything which concerns us. Therefore we have a right to talk with Him about all things, and to speak with Him very plainly too, for there is no virtue in obscurity and circumlocution in a personal conference.

Practical Needs

Suppose, for example, that a mother is reading these words—that she has four children, that her husband is dead, that she has no income except what she derives from her labor as a scrubwoman or a seamstress, that it is the dead of winter, that her fuel is exhausted and that her children are crying from hunger and cold. Suppose, further, that in the providence of God she has no friends in the place where she is. Suppose she is alone in a great city and does not know anyone to whom she can turn. What shall we tell the woman respecting prayer?

We ought to tell her that God, who hears the ravens and the young lions and provides for the needs of these creatures, knows all about her, is interested in her, and that she has a right to talk with Him very simply and plainly. She can say "coal" and "bread" and "milk" and "eggs" and "snow" and "ice" and "storm" with the assurance that He understands exactly what she is talking about, and that He is both able and disposed to minister to her immediate needs.

Suppose that it be a case of sickness or an alienated friendship. God's people need to know and practically to believe that there is no need of any kind which comes to them concerning which they may not speak to Him with perfect freedom. There are no little things in our lives when we come to look at them thoroughly, and God wishes us to be perfectly frank and free in our conversations with Him.

When a friend leaves us for a journey, we should pray for wisdom that he may keep out of the way of trains, may not be run down by streetcars, may not be crushed by some fast-flying automobile. We ought to pray for engineers and firemen, for conductors and porters, for passengers and for passersby. We ought to thank God for our houses, and to pray Him to protect them from fire and wind and wicked men and evil angels. The more childlike we are in approaching God, the more certain we are to avail ourselves of the privileges which He has put within our power.

Victory Over Temptations

The Bible speaks of being "in heaviness through manifold temptations"; it also speaks of "resisting unto blood, striving against sin." The example of our Lord in the wilderness shows that temptations from Satan may be so terrible as to cause one to go without food for forty days without experiencing hunger. Satan, who did not hesitate to assail the Lord Jesus Himself, is not likely to be afraid of any of His followers. In fact, all who know even a little of the Christian life will testify that there is no affliction or trial more terrible than temptation to sin.

God delivers men from temptation in many ways. I remember at one time in my life when I was most fiercely assailed by Satan. It seemed I could do nothing but pray constantly that God would deliver me from the power of evil and enable me to live a holy life.

When the assaults of Satan and my prayers were at their height, I was suddenly taken sick. I was more sick than I had been for many years, and the sickness continued for some time.

I did not immediately associate it with my prayers or with the temptations which I had been experiencing. But when I had passed the crisis of the disease and was able to think a little, I was surprised to observe how completely the temptations with which I had been struggling had passed away. They seemed like a dark, unlovely memory that had no apparent relation to my present being.

When this had become clear in my consciousness, I recalled the prayers I had been uttering and especially remembered the energy with which those prayers had risen at the time I was stricken down.

Sometimes God delivers His people from temptation by the presence and help of other people. At times the relief from the power of temptation will be conscious and obvious. At other times the relief will not appear to be what it is until the time is passed.

The disposition of our Heavenly Father to deliver us from the power of evil is known to all Christian people. The methods in which He works our salvation are numberless. Prayer is probably involved in them all. When you are tempted to sin you may be delivered, if you will wait upon God.

Failures in Christian living are the sources of doubts, fears, discouragement, and uselessness. Every holy life is a continuous power working with God for the salvation of the world. Satan is willing that we should believe, if he can only render our belief ineffective by reason of our defects. Therefore we "ought always to pray, and not to faint."

Healing

Years ago, being oftentimes a guest in homes where people were kind to me and where there were sick ones, I felt sad that I had not the gift of the early Christian teachers so that I might heal the sick in homes where I was a guest. I finally spoke to the Lord respecting this matter, asking that if it was His will I might, in some small way, be a benefit to good people who were afflicted in their bodies.

Shortly after I began to offer this petition God gave me the privilege of praying with a friend in New York City. He had been consulting all the physicians he thought could help him, and had steadily grown worse. His wife was in his office trying to carry on his work. He was sorely perplexed, not knowing which way to turn or what to do. He, his wife, and I were permitted to pray in the Tribune Building for the rebuke of the disease and for the healing of this sick man. God was pleased to send healing. He immediately began to recover, before long came to his usual strength, and has been for years transacting business in that office.

Not a great while after this, in the city of Chicago, I was a guest in a home where the wife was almost dying with rheumatism and other ailments. She also had had the best medical attendance, and was not better, but, on the other hand, grew worse. Her husband, she, and I knelt in the dining room where the conversation respecting her efforts to secure medical aid had taken place, and she also speedily recovered. I was in that home within a week or ten days, and found her looking well and strong, moving freely and happily about the home.

In our own hometown, Wheaton, some time after this, there was living a friend who was an elder in the first church to which I had the privilege of preaching statedly. His wife was seriously ill; age was against her; the physicians did not seem able to help her. Her children were called in to see her die and remained for several days awaiting the end.

Under these circumstances I was requested to call and have prayer with her and her husband. I did so, and it pleased God to recover her. The children who had come to see her die went home; she began again to go about the house. That was a number of years since, but at last reports she was quite well. These are not the only instances in which I have been permitted to see healing after prayer.

Someone may say, "Have you never seen prayer offered, or made it yourself, for the sick when they failed to recover?" Yes, repeatedly. No one should believe that God has put the power of life and death out of His own hands. But that it has pleased God to hear prayer for the sick in many instances I personally know. What is most remarkable and comforting is the fact that in these cases, as a rule, not one or two but many physicians had been consulted and had been unable to help.

Prayer for Rain

I have spoken to some readers hitherto of our family prayers for rain. We never offered these prayers until there was imperative need. We never offered them until we were, as we believed, led by the Spirit to do so. We never offered them except at times when there had been long disappointment and when there was no present sign of relief; but in every case these family prayers, in which all joined, from the youngest to myself, were followed by showers from heaven.

I desire to mention one instance which has never been printed, and which differs from those which I have referred to.

We were, at one time, in the midst of a serious drought. It had continued for weeks, and there was no token of relief. After luncheon one day, as I left the dining room, I was deeply impressed that I should go into my room and pray for rain. I did so, going alone and saying nothing to anyone of the burden which had been laid upon me. It was about two o'clock in the afternoon that I felt the assurance that rain would come.

I went from my room, and in front of our home met Mrs. Blanchard, and said to her, "I have just been moved to pray for rain." At that time there was, so far as I could tell, no more sign of rain than there had been during the weeks of drought, but at five o'clock that afternoon refreshing showers came pouring down upon the earth.

In Wheaton some years before, prayers were offered at a public meeting called for the purpose of prayer for rain. Before the meeting was adjourned, the showers had come.

One may ask again, "But have not you and have not friends prayed for rain when it did not come?" In a general way, yes; in a particular and definite way, no. I do not remember a time when we have made a special, definite appeal to God for rain that it has not come.

Always when we began these prayers we confessed our Sabbath-breaking, our neglect of God's Word, our failure to use property with an eye single to His glory, our vanity, our pride, our self-righteousness, our ill desert. I do not believe it is possible to get gifts from God in answer to prayer, without humility of heart and confession of sin. If God were to bestow answers to prayer on proud, self-righteous, sinning people, He would offer a premium on negligence, carelessness, and evildoing.

In place of thinking it strange that God does not do more for us in the way of temporal blessings, I am astonished that He does not destroy us when I think of our national sins—prayer meetings neglected; lodges, theaters and dancing halls full; the Bible put aside; newspapers, magazines, and wretched novels occupying the attention and time of professed Christians. Is it not a marvel, things being as they are, that God can answer prayer at all?

Prayer for the College

I began work in Wheaton College in September of 1872. Since that time, in the midst of many imperfections and failures, I have given myself to the service of the kingdom of God among the young people of my country and time.

Almost all the graduates of the College during these years have, before completing their courses, confessed themselves believers in Jesus Christ. A large number, something like forty percent of the men graduates, have given themselves to the ministry, to service as Christian teachers in home and foreign lands, to work in the Young Men's Christian Association, or some other form of Christian service.

We began with almost nothing in the way of money, and have never had, from the beginning until now, a wealthy patron who made the College his first care. Our helpers have been broad-minded, largehearted men and women who gave what they gave to the College, not for personal glory but for the sake of the work it was seeking to do. They were givers in many directions, and did not feel that they wished to make one institution their chief care. One of them said to me, when I asked him if he would not consider making the College his chief work, "I am giving now to one hundred different charities, and I do not dare or wish to cut off one." The result has been that oftentimes we have been in sore need of money.

I have been so encouraged in my work and prayers by the example of George Müller. Only this morning I read about his work at Bristol where many hundreds of orphans are fed and clothed and educated and launched on life. For tens of years it has been the rule that the daily needs had a daily supply and nothing more. When they required a building, God sent the money for a building. When they wanted a breakfast, God sent the money for the breakfast, but there was little or nothing left over for dinner or supper—oftentimes nothing at all, so that Mr. Müller said, "Not once, nor twice, nor scores of times, but literally, hundreds of times when one meal was eaten there was not either the food or money to secure the next one for about two thousand orphans."

That has been the way God has cared for them; but about six months ago [just before the start of World War I] the orphanages unexpectedly found themselves with money on hand for some six months in advance. How did this happen? Did it *happen* or was it a divine provision for a time of stress about which men at that time knew absolutely nothing? There was not a statesman in the world at that time who could have foretold the way in which money and men would have been drained out of England and other lands for the awful war which is on. But the same God who could supply a dinner when breakfast had been eaten, can equally well supply for six months in advance, or six years, or sixty years, or six hundred years, if He pleases. What man puts a shovelful of coal on a fire without using a provision for a need which God had anticipated for thousands of years?

Is it not strange that we pray as poorly as we do? Ought we not continually to pray for wisdom and strength to pray? How wise if, day by day, we should come to our loving Saviour, saying to Him, "Lord, teach us to pray." How greatly are we encouraged thus to do when we remember tht He did not reprove His defective, imperfect disciples because they could not pray better, but right away said to them, "When ye pray, say, 'Our Father, which art in heaven' " (Luke 11:2).

PART FOUR

HOW DOES GOD ANSWER PRAYER?

You may have used the words "surrender" and "consecration" many times, but without rightly understanding what they mean. As you have been brought by the teaching of Romans 7 to a complete sense of the hopelessness of leading a true Christian life, or a true prayer life, by your own efforts, so you feel that the Lord Jesus must take you up, by His own power, in an entirely new way; and must take possession of you, by His Spirit, in an entirely new measure. This alone can preserve you from constantly sinning afresh. This only can make you really victorious. This leads you to look away from yourself, really to get free from yourself, and to expect everything from the Lord Jesus.

If we begin to understand this, we are prepared to admit that in our nature there is nothing good, that it is under a curse, and is nailed with Christ to His cross. We come to see what Paul means when he says that we are dead to sin by the death of Christ. Thus do we obtain a share of the glorious resurrection life there is in Him. By such an insight we are encouraged to believe that Christ, through His life in us, through His continual indwelling, can keep us. Just as, at our conversion, we had no rest till we knew He had received us—so now we feel the need of coming to Him, to receive from Him the assurance that He has really undertaken to keep us by the power of His resurrection life.

Andrew Murray

CHAPTER NINETEEN

GOD CHANGES
THOSE WHO PRAY

Some persons do not believe that God answers prayer by bestowing things asked. They teach that the value of prayer is that it changes our attitudes. They look upon it like the exercises of a gymnasium, which are not intended to be fruitful except in the lives of those who take them.

It is safe to say that there never has been a prevailing belief of any kind which does not contain some elements of truth. The above is a partial statement of the facts in the case. It does change men to pray and the change which is wrought in them is one of the ways in which God answers their prayers.

Men who believe that God answers prayer look on praying as the farmer does on his plowing, sowing, and reaping. He plows and sows and reaps not for exercise, not to put his body in condition, but to get wheat or oats or rye.

The old divines divided prayer into adoration, confession, submission, petition and thanksgiving. Every one of these states of mind is an essential element of real prayer, and each one of them naturally tends to the securing of all sorts of good by the one who prays.

Adoration

Suppose that I am in need of money and I ask God to give me money. I really pray for it. I ask for it in the name of Jesus. I ask for it with thanksgiving. I ask for it with submission. I ask for it with fixed contemplation of the being and attributes of God. I adore Him.

What must be the spiritual effect of time spent in this manner? Beyond doubt it clarifies my mind, it unburdens my heart, it stimulates all my energies, it puts me in condition for effective service. It rejuvenates. Going from such a season of prayer, I naturally take hold of my business in a more effective manner than was possible when my mind was fixed on lesser things. Such a time of waiting before God happifies, and this in itself tends to secure favor from men and opportunities to advance. No duty in human life can be performed as well when I am dwelling upon the petty, upon the imperfect, as it can when I am meditating on the character and work of God. It is therefore true that prayer is a spiritual gymnastic. It is far more than this, but this it certainly is, and this is one way in which God answers our prayers.

Confession

Nothing cripples like unconfessed sin. There are ten thousand men walking the streets of any great city today, burdened and unfit for going on, simply because they have neglected or refused to confess their faults, their sins. The reason why men, who have been far gone in sin, are so filled with gladness when they are saved, is because as a rule they very frankly and fully confess their shortcomings. Men who have lived outwardly decent lives are oftentimes held back from this kind of confession. Men whose characters and reputations have been destroyed, who have become ragged and filthy because of their sinful lives, are saved from the temptation to cover up their sins. Their evildoings are obvious. The world knows them for what they have been, and when Jesus changes them they do not attempt to hide the fact that they owe a great debt for a tremendous salvation.

David said that when he kept silence his bones waxed old through his sorrow all the day long (Ps. 32:3). But when he made confession of his sin, he came into condition for service again. "Restore unto me the joy of Thy salvation. . . . Then will I teach transgressors Thy ways" (Ps 51:12-13).

That is, when the joy of salvation returned, he could go to work for God and for himself. It is difficult for most men to confess their sins.

Francis Murphy, the great temperance advocate, said, "The three most difficult words to pronounce in the English language are, 'I was wrong.' " These three words are not only difficult—they are fundamentally important. If men will not acknowledge their sins, God cannot grant their requests. Many years ago I heard a minister say, "If there is a piece of lead weighing a pound at the bottom of a pitcher, you may pump the Atlantic Ocean into that pitcher, but you cannot fill it until you take the lead out." Just so, there are sins in the lives of men that lie in the memory as a dark and heavy thing. The hearts of such persons can never be filled with joy and peace, they can never be fit to do their own work or to do God's work until the "lead" is removed by an honest confession. Confession is wonderful and it works.

Men who will confess their sins can make advances, and men who will not confess their sins can make no solid advances. The meditation on the character and attributes of God naturally leads us to think of our own shortcomings, misgivings, failures. If we are frank and free in speaking of them to God, we enter into the state of peace and rest, and coming into this state, we are ready for anything. We can do or suffer triumphantly when the conscience has been cleared by honest confession and the blood of Christ.

Submission

Another thing which prayer does for men is to bring them into a state of honest and happy submission to God. When men reflect upon what God is and what they are, and honestly confess their own failures in view of God's character, they naturally find it easy to submit to the will of God. This is another source of peace, of restfulness, and when we rest, we gather energy and become fit. It is safe to say that one of the most common sources of weakness and incapacity is a restless fretting, a secret rebellion against the will and plan of God.

Here is a mother praying for a sick child, and she really

prays. She adores; she confesses. By and by she will come to submit, if she continues to adore and to confess, and when she really submits, when she comes to say, "Not my will, but Thine," she will be a thousand times more competent to care for her sick child than when she is rebelling, even unconsciously, against the plan of God. Her own nerves will quiet, her eyesight will clear. Her courage will stay and by the very change produced in herself, it is entirely possible that God may save the life of her child.

Take the case of a man who desires a certain position. His motives are mixed. There is an element of the divine. There is an element of the human. The position is attractive, the compensation may be large, the associations may be desirable. At the same time, opportunity for service may be great and the man himself may find these varying motives so entangled that he cannot exactly say which one is predominant. But coming before God for this position which he desires, he thinks of God as Maker and Ruler of the universe, as high and holy and lifted up. He thinks of himself as sinful by nature, as having oftentimes added to the sinfulness of his nature the guilt of actual transgression. He becomes submissive. He puts himself at the disposal of God. He consents to what the providence of God shall reveal. Cannot anyone see that under these circumstances the man is more likely to secure what he deserves than if, with a stiff neck and a high head and an unsubmissive heart, he were to struggle for it? The very state of mind into which he comes will—if you allow the expression—make it more possible for God to give the thing which he desires.

Petition

It is petition which is the principal element in prayer, though the other items which have been mentioned are, either in conscious or unconscious form, necessary precedent conditions. But if there is no request, there is no prayer. Meditation upon the character of God, upon our own characters and humble submission to God inclines us to ask things from Him and enables us joyfully and perseveringly to do so. "Ye have not, because ye ask not" (James 4:2). The Holy Spirit thus recorded the failure of first-century Christians who thought they prayed. This difficulty still remains. The poet says,

Prayer is the soul's sincere desire,
Uttered or unexpressed.

But sincere desire does not mean simply wanting things. It means desiring things when we have in mind the greatness and goodness of God, our own ill desert, and a humble willingness to receive the thing that God chooses to send. All men do not desire the same things. The differences between men are very largely in their desires, and their desires are occasioned by their characters. Men desire different things because they are different persons; and men who desire with a proper thought of God, desire and ask in a totally different manner from that employed by other sorts of people.

Some do not ask because they are too proud. They do not realize the difference between themselves and God. Some do not ask because they rely upon their own efforts to secure the thing which they desire. Some do not ask because they are not in condition to ask. A child in rebellion against his father will never be free in his petitions. But a loving child who knows the power and goodness of his father, and his own helplessness, and who is willing that his father should do what he wills, is in good condition to make requests. I can testify from experience that it is very difficult to refuse the request of such a child.

"Ye have not, because ye ask not." What a complete explanation of the failure of the prayer life of people, as well as of their failures in other respects. I do not think that the Holy Spirit was speaking through James of unsaved people. Most of the Bible was written for persons who were right with God. The Bible message to an unrepentant sinner is very short. "Repent, and believe the Gospel" is pretty much all that he needs to hear. But we children, babes in the house of God, need to learn to walk, to talk, to take hold of things. We need to come into the stature of the fullness of Christ (Eph. 4:13).

This is why there is so much reproof, so much example,

so much encouragement for us in the Word of God. This is why we are reminded that we fail to receive things because we fail to ask. I am sure that I have a thousand times failed to receive good gifts from God, because I did not ask. In many of these cases, my failure was thoughtlessness, natural impulse to work myself, a failure to adore, to confess and to submit, all of which would naturally have led me to ask for the things which I needed and really desired rather than to seek to obtain them for myself.

Thanksgiving

God answers prayer by working changes in us, among other things. These changes are not chance happenings, but are wrought in accordance with the laws by which He governs the material and spiritual world. The soul which adores, which confesses failure, which offers up its submission and which makes its requests to God, will have abundant occasions for thanksgiving.

> Nor is the least a thankful heart,
> Which takes those gifts with joy.

Indeed, this is one of the great gifts of God, a thankful heart. We often assume the things which require most care, and many times we care for things which may be assumed. How many times have you heard a person pray for grace to be grateful? How many times have you prayed for power to sympathize? How many times have you prayed for a praiseful heart? Sam Jones used to say that there were two parts to man's relations to God—man's part and God's part. He said men are all the while assuming that their part is well done and they are very much afraid that God will fail in His; whereas the fact is that God never fails at all, that the failure, if there is any, is on our part.

At the funeral of a little child, I heard a brother minister say, "Lord, teach us to sympathize." It was a helpful word to me. I saw that I did not know how. I knew a dear saint who lived a long life under circumstances of great tribulation, whose habit it was to begin her testimony in the prayer meeting with the words, "I pray for strength to praise my God." These are wise words and it would be eminently wise if we should pray more than we do for thankful hearts and for the gift of expressing our thankfulness. While this duty is preeminently one which we owe to God, it is also a duty to the many about us who contribute to our well-being. I wish that into the lives of all who read these words there might come *a storm of thanksgiving*.

I am sure that one of the griefs of God and good people is that men so seldom and in such stinted fashion express the thanksgiving which perhaps in a blind, halfhearted way they feel. What husband is there who does not owe his wife ten thousand thanksgivings for the patient, loving service of years? What wife does not at times cause her husband to wonder whether she really does appreciate the patient labor that brings the comforts into the home for her and her children? What parent is there who has not a right at times to think that his children do not appreciate the loving care which has watched over them from the beginning in their homes? What children are there who do not render ten thousand little services to father and mother, for which they receive scanty, if any, thanks at all?

Once when I was leading a special meeting for a few weeks, I said to the young people, "We have prayed a good deal first and last. Let us make this meeting a thanksgiving meeting." And I went through the hymnbook which we were using at that time to select praiseful hymns. As I recall, there were something like three hundred hymns in that book and I had hard work to find a dozen that were really hymns of praise. There were lots of prayers, there were lots of exhortations, there were a great number of sentimental ditties of one kind and another. But real praise to God for His patient forbeariang love and His ceaseless, watchful care, was almost wanting.

Is not this enough to break the heart even of the Almighty, that there is such a stinted return for the unnumbered blessings He pours upon us? And is this not one of the evils in our lives which is cured by prayer? For prayer brings us into a state of mind and heart where we are fitted to do life's work and to receive God's goodness in some way that shall accomplish what the will of God desires.

Oh, think over the holiness of God, and bow in lowliness before Him, till your heart is filled with the assurance of what the Holy One will do for you. Take a week, if necessary, to read and reread the words of God on this great truth, till your heart is brought under the conviction: "This is the glory of the inner chamber, to converse with God the Holy One; to bow in deep humility and shame before Him, because we have so despised Him and His love through our prayerlessness." There we shall receive the assurance that He will again take us into fellowship with Himself. No one can expect to understand and receive the holiness of God who is not often and long alone with God.

Someone has said that the holiness of God is the expression of the unspeakable distance by which He in His righteousness is separated from us, and yet also of the unspeakable nearness in which He in His love longs to hold fellowship with us, and dwell in us. Bow in humble reverence, as you think of the immeasurable distance between you and God. Bow in childlike confidence in the unspeakable desire of His love to be united with you in the deepest intimacy; and reckon most confidently on Him to reveal something of His holiness to the soul which thirsts after Him, and waits upon Him, and is quiet before Him.

Andrew Murray

CHAPTER TWENTY

GOD DIRECTS US TO SOURCES OF HELP

A very dear friend of mine, who is a successful physician, told me that early in his career he was called to visit a little girl who was critically ill. He said that he honestly cared for her as well as he knew how, and yet every day it seemed that she was marching steadily down to the grave. He was distressed on many counts. It was hard to see the little thing suffer; it was hard to see the sufferings of her parents. He knew that if she should die it would be mentioned to his discredit as a physician. There would be a loss of reputation and a consequent loss of income. For all these reasons and others, he desired that the little girl might recover. Everything which he knew how to do, he did, and all seemed unavailing.

In this state of mind and heart he went into his back office, shut the door and locked it, and kneeling before God, said to Him, "Father, please show me what that little girl needs. I do not know how to help her." Waiting there before God, his mind was directed to a remedy of which he had read, but which he had never known to be employed. Rising from his knees, he went at once and prepared a portion of that remedy. Calling a messenger, he sent it to the house with directions to throw away all the medicines which he had left and employ this one. It was the one thing in the universe of God which was prepared for a human body suffering in the particular way in which that little child was afflicted.

At once there was improvement and improvement passed on to complete recovery, to the joy and help of all concerned.

H.L. Hastings of Boston, author of lectures on the Bible, and editor for many years of *The Christian*, told me that at one time his wife was sick and near to death. Prayer was offered without ceasing and apparently without avail. Remedies which seemed appropriate were used but all were apparently useless. Step by step she went down toward death. In a great agony of spirit he went apart to pray, and as he prayed he remembered that he had heard that flour, browned in a pan, could be retained by the stomach when nothing else could be. His wife had for days been so that even clear water was instantly rejected, and she was lying as one without any hope, physically speaking.

After having prepared this browned flour, he gave her a small portion from a teaspoon, and she retained it. Shortly thereafter he gave her more which also she retained. It was the beginning of a complete recovery. I suppose she lived thirty years after that time. I myself held meetings with her and her son after the death of Mr. Hastings. She was then in vigorous life and greatly used in work for the kingdom of God.

Human Agency

In another chapter I have spoken of two mottoes, the one, "Trust God," the other, "Trust God, and tell His children." Both Hudson Taylor and George Müller believed in informing the Lord's people respecting the work committed to them. The question was whether, having given the information, they should then say to one or more of the Lord's people, "We should be glad of your assistance in this enterprise," or should leave the Holy Spirit to direct Christians interested to such conclusions as He desired them to make.

Let me say that as in the case of healing, so in the case of provision for temporal needs, I hold that all that is accomplished in any good work is from God. It is true that if men solicit money, and if in answer to their requests moneys are given, some persons will attribute the result to the men. This has always seemed to me a foolish proceeding and a sort of atheism and blasphemy, for all persons who are fairly intelligent about such work know that there are hundreds and thousands of cases where men do solicit unavailingly. There are other cases where solicitation is wonderfully effective; the results are a surprise to both parties, very many times to the solicitor, many times to the solicited.

What now makes the difference between the cases where the result is favorable and those instances where it is unfavorable? We must take God into the account here. Certainly I do, and if a man tells me that he has raised a certain sum of money, I always feel as I do when a doctor tells me that he has healed a sick person. I do not believe that any doctor ever healed any sick person, or ever will, and I do not believe that any good man ever raised money for a good cause, himself alone considered. All our works are wrought in God. "Every good gift and every perfect gift is from above, and cometh down from the Father of lights, with whom is no variableness, neither shadow of turning" (James 1:17). How absurd to the verge of blasphemy for men to attribute the favorable results of their activities to themselves!

We all believe that in order to raise corn and wheat men should plow and plant and sow and cultivate and gather in. This is a commonplace. We all know that if men do efficiently and faithfully what they are directed to do in these particulars, God frequently, shall I say usually, rewards their toil. It is His mode of administration. He likes to see men industrious and He likes to reward industry and He does. He places no premiums on laziness and He is offended with presumption. Would it have been good a thing for Mr. Hastings, when the Holy Spirit reminded him of roasted flour, to remain on his knees, praying God to heal his wife? I think if he had done so Mrs. Hastings would have died at that time. It seems to me that the Holy Spirit told him to brown the flour and give it to her, and a failure of obedience would, like any other failure, have resulted in disaster.

I remember some years ago when we were in great need of money at the College. We needed it for almost everything and so far as we could see, there was nothing before us but need. Under these circumstances a gentleman mentioned to me a lady living in Madison, Wisconsin. I had never heard of her but he said that she was a good woman, that she had means and that she was generous. I sat down and wrote a brief letter, telling her as well as I could our situation, and soliciting her interest. She replied immediately that she had no funds available at that time but that she was interested and thought that she might thereafter become a helper.

It was only a little time before I received word from her attorney that she had made an appropriation of $1,000 for this work. I prayed in those days as I do now—I try to pray without ceasing. In some measure I think God has taught me how to do this, not so fully and perfectly as I hope He will, but in some measure. Would it have been an exhibition of faith and obedience if I had said to myself when this lady was mentioned to me, or had said to my friend, "I pray God to help. I do not believe in talking to people. If God wishes her to assist us, she will hear of us in some way and will do it"? I do not believe that this would have been pleasing to God, but I do not for an instant attribute her gift to my own exertions. I do not admit that the work was in any respect less than the work of God because I did what I think He told me to do in the premises.

I remember when I was praying for the recovery of Mrs. Blanchard, who had been for quite a while seriously ill, and the Holy Spirit said to me, "Have you confessed your faults?"

I said, "No."

He then asked me if I would do it, and I told him, "Yes."

Supposing I had declined to obey Him—could I have hoped for her healing? I do not think so. I do not wish anyone to receive the impression that I doubt God's ability and His frequent disposition to help people directly. I think I have made myself sufficiently clear in regard to this point.

God Chooses Variety

I believe that sick people are healed, that moneys are secured, that human hearts are changed oftentimes with no human interposition of any kind whatsoever. When human agency is impossible, we are shut up to prayer. When human agency is possible, and the Holy Spirit directs us to employ it, I think we should do so, always remembering that all our works are wrought of God.

Take the case of one who prays for sanctification and who becomes sanctified, who secures victory over the world, the flesh, and Satan. How will it be attained? In many instances, no doubt, by the direct impulse of the Holy Spirit; at other times, probably, by direction to sources of help which may properly be employed. In each case the work is wrought of God, in one case by one means, in another case by another means.

The different methods which Christ employed in the healing of the blind have always seemed to me significant of His general plan. In one case, He spoke to a blind man and sight came into his eyes. In another case, He touched the eyes of a blind man and spoke, and he saw. In another case, He touched the eyes of a blind man once and he saw imperfectly. He touched them again and he saw perfectly. In still another case, He made clay out of the dust and placed that upon the blind man's eyes and sent him to wash in the pool of Siloam, and he went and washed and came seeing.

No one who believes Jesus Christ to be God can doubt His ability to have healed these four persons in the same manner, yet He chose four methods. Why? I think among other reasons to teach us that He is not shut up to single ways of doing things—that He chooses variety. He puts this in nature. Study the clouds in a summer sky and see how continually they change. Study the flowers in a meadow. Look at the reds, the blues, the pinks, the yellows, the scarlets. Study the leaves, not only on the different trees, but on a single tree. How impossible to find two which exactly correspond. Look at the fields. See the green, the light green, the dark green, the yellow. Study the trees of the forest. See the beeches, the maples, the poplars, the oaks, the elms, the hemlocks, the pines, the cypress. Here is an absolutely endless variety. Why? Because it pleases God to make it.

I am inclined to think He likes to see it just as I do. He

says that men are created in His image. I imagine that the things which please us in this wonderful world please Him, that He rejoices in His works as His children do. If this is true in the world of things, how much more true in the world of rational beings. Frequently when I hear men talk about prayer, they lay down rules and methods. They want us to pray in this way and in that way. They tell us how they have prayed, how other people have prayed, and running through the whole of their teaching there is a strong undertone of, "Go thou, and do likewise." I do not find anything of the sort in God's Word. I do not believe this is the divine mind.

It is true that we are to be followers of those who through faith and patience have inherited the promises. It is also true that as many as are led by the Spirit of God are the sons of God, and that all the sons of God have a right to be led by the Spirit of God. I do not try to pray like anybody else. I try to pray the way God wishes me to pray. Someone may say, "Well, that is a lazy way to do. If you would pray for hours and hours, if you would pray all night or all day, you would get on with your work far better than you do." Possibly it is true—I am not sure; but I shall never try to pray all night because somebody else did. The example of Jesus does have weight. The example of good men has weight, but the only teacher who can teach me infallibly is the Spirit of God.

If He tells me to pray all night, I shall try to do it as faithfully as I can. If He tells me to pray for two hours, I will do that. I do not doubt that occasionally in a public meeting the Holy Spirit tells men to pray at length. My observation has led me to believe that long prayers in the midst of public assemblies are almost always a blunder. I believe they are very seldom divinely ordained.

I have real sympathy with Mr. Moody's action when at one time a man was praying for all creation in a public meeting and Mr. Moody finally said, "Let us now sing the sixty-third hymn, while the brother is finishing his prayer." It was not an irreverence; it was not a discourtesy. It was a relief of a long-suffering congregation—a needed relief, and I believe that it did good to all concerned, including the man who was praying.

I heard Mr. Moody once say another thing which I have always remembered.

Men generally pray in public
in inverse proportion to their private prayers.
If they pray a great deal in private,
they are apt to be rather short in public prayer.
If they pray very little in private,
they are in danger of being more lengthy.

I do not say that this is a rule; I do not believe in any rule for prayer except the rule which I have indicated. Praying in the Holy Ghost is the only safe thing for any man to undertake. Persons who do this will pray wisely and God will direct them to the things which they ought to do, and this is one way in which He will answer their prayers. I believe there are many people who, as they read these words, will respond to them with an affirmation that this is the manner in which God has at times aided them.

To understand grace, to understand Christ aright, we must understand what sin is. And how otherwise can we come to this understanding than through the light of God and His Word?

Come with me to the beginning of the Bible. See there man created by God, after His image, and pronounced by His Creator to be very good. Then sin entered, as rebellion against God. Adam was driven out of Paradise, and was brought along with the untold millions of following generations under curse and ruin. That was the work of sin. Here we learn its nature and power.

Come further on, and see the ark of Noah on Ararat. So terrible had godlessness become among men, God saw nothing for it but to destroy man from off the earth. That was the work of sin.

Come once more with me, to Sinai. God wished to establish His covenant with a new nation—with the people of Israel. But because of man's sinfulness, He can do this only by appearing in darkness and lightning so terrible that Moses said, "I exceedingly fear and quake." And before the end of the giving of the Law, that awful message came: "Cursed is every one that continueth not in all things, which are written in the Book of the Law to do them." It was sin which made that necessary. *Andrew Murray*

CHAPTER TWENTY-ONE

GOD CHANGES
THE ORDER OF NATURE

I t is a most remarkable fact that anyone who professes to be a Christian should ever doubt God's power to change the order of nature. It is safe to say that those who have this impression have never really understood what is involved or they would either cease to call themselves Christians, or cease to doubt the wonder-working power of God. The alternative of theism is atheism, pantheism, polytheism. Any false faith when fairly tested will appear to be simply the denial of the existence of God. False gods are not gods, and since the mind as well as the universe at large is constructed on the basis of truth, they must in the end appear to be what they are. When a man doubts God to be what He has represented Himself to be, in his *heart* he is saying, "No God." With his *head* he tries to say, "There is no God," and with his *lips*, occasionally he arrives at this depth of depravity.

Can He Do It?

It is a blunder to discuss details when the establishing of the general principle will settle all. The atonement, the resurrection of Jesus, real conversions—people make these the subject of detailed and exhaustive inquiry.

The fundamental question is as to the supernatural. Who made the universe? Is it a result of chance? Did it happen to be as it is, with its marvelous order, with its wonderful evidences of design, or did it have an intelligent, all-powerful Creator? If the world was made by God, did God put it beyond His power? If He created the world and launched it on its career, could He cause it to pause if He desired? If He creates millions of human beings under the laws of ordinary descent, could He create beings otherwise if He chose? If He causes the world to spring into new life every year and day, and makes dull earth exhibit forms of beauty on every side, could He speak life into the body of a man who had ceased to breathe?

It is a matter of great amazement that persons who call themselves theists, to say nothing of Christians, should pick flaws in one miracle or another as if it were a great marvel. Why do not such persons declare themselves atheists at once? Perhaps because salaries are involved. Perhaps because atheism has rather a bad reputation. Perhaps because they are simply defective in their methods of thought. Yet these people should understand that if they wish to affect the public mind, they must attain to at least some degree of sequence in thinking.

The person who doubts the possibility of miracles is simply an atheist. For if there is a God, then certainly He will work like a God. It is natural for every being to act according to his own character.

He Might, But Will He?

This is a question not as to the power but as to the disposition of God. All except atheists believe that God *can* interfere with the administration of the universe if He pleases. But will He do it? This depends upon need and disposition.

Suppose a widow has two sons and they are about to be led into slavery because she cannot pay her debts. She has no natural means of securing the money. God could supply it any way He pleases. He could direct some person who has it to bring it to her. He could open a vein of gold on the side of a hill just as He opens a spring of water. There is no more supernatural power required in the one case than in the other. He could multiply oil in a vessel as easily as He can increase oil in a tree. But will He do this? That depends on the need and on His disposition. If the woman has need and if God is disposed to supply it, certainly He will supply it. But in what way will He supply it? In whatever way He chooses. One man says, "I should think He would supply it in this way," and another man says, "I should think He would supply it in that way." God will not take counsel of either one but will supply the need, if He so wills, in His own way.

He Might, But Does He?

We are now not on a question of disposition or power but of evidence. It is alleged that God has interfered with the order of nature repeatedly, that He has caused sick people, who would naturally require a good while to get well even if they did not die, to be recovered in an instant of time. It is reported that He has cleansed lepers by a touch and a word, that He has opened the eyes of men born blind and enabled men hopelessly crippled to walk and run and leap. It is declared that He has quickened into life a child who had been dead for an hour, a young man who had been dead for half a day, another young man who had lain in the grave for three days. There is no argument among Christians, not even among theists, as to the possibility of this. There is no discussion among Christians as to God's disposition to do work of this kind, provided there were sufficient need.

We are now in the region of evidence—testimony. We know some things through our senses—we see, smell, touch, or taste. We know other things through consciousness. We enjoy, suffer, remember, imagine, hope, fear, and we know that we do these things. We have some knowledge derived from reason apart from the senses or from consciousness. We know that space is without bounds, that duration is without end, that causes produce results, that results are produced by causes. We know that causes must be adequate. We know that they must be appropriate.

If a man tells us that one morning in the Alps, he picked up Mount Blanc and threw it over into the Mediterranean Sea, we know that this is not true. We know that the assigned cause is not equal to the alleged effect. Most of us know the interior of Africa by another's testimony, if at all. We have never been there. Consciousness tells us nothing about it. Reason tells us nothing about it. Admiral Peary said that there was a certain piece of land in the Arctic regions. This year explorers are said to have gone to that point and found an ocean. Either Mr. Peary did not tell what was true, or the patch of land which he said existed in that quarter of the globe disappeared between the time of his visit and the investigation of this year. But we depend upon testimony. We have the right to depend upon testimony.

The Value of Testimony

The value of testimony depends upon the competence, the integrity, the interest, and the number of witnesses. An unlettered plowman cannot tell us about our distance from the sun. A skilled astronomer who has never farmed cannot tell us the best methods of raising corn. Each man is entitled to bear testimony to what he knows and to nothing else. A liar is not believed, nor is a man of no integrity or character. We believe some men when they make the most absurd statements because we know them to be men of stern integrity. We doubt other men's statements which are not in themselves at all improbable, simply because we know the men are untruthful. As between persons of these two sorts giving opposite testimony, we always and necessarily believe the man of solid character. We have to believe him. We are so constructed that we cannot avoid it, and we do not believe the other man. We are so constructed that we cannot believe him even if we wish to.

It is also in evidence that the personal interest of witnesses has much to do with the value of their testimony. If I make a certain statement for which I receive ten thousand dollars in gold, my testimony may be very true, but it is not so forceful as it would be if I made the same statement, knowing that for the making I should lose all that I possess. If a man testifies with the known probability that he will be imprisoned, perhaps crucified, his testimony is more valuable than would be the testimony of another person on the same subject, who, because of his testimony, would receive the gifts of houses and lands. These are commonplaces, but they are oftentimes forgotten by people who speak on religious subjects.

If people who write books on prayer, on the authenticity and integrity of the Scriptures, were subject to cross-examination as are witnesses in a human court, we should be spared a lot of folly which now cumbers bookshelves for a while and then goes back to the paper makers. It is obvious that the testimony of a dozen witnesses of good character is more weighty than the testimony of one witness of good character. One man may be mistaken regarding the question of fact when he is sincerely endeavoring to state the exact truth. A dozen persons might be mistaken, but the probabilities of error in the latter case are very few comparatively.

Does God Interfere in the Order of Nature?

My gifts are those of the teacher. I never had the gift of prophecy, nor the gift of healing, nor the distinctive gifts of a pastor. Without my desire, without even my thought, God called me into the high and holy office of a teacher. In that office He has continued me for more than fifty years since I taught my first public school in Cook County, Illinois. I praise Him for this high honor. In my work as a teacher I have been a guest in many homes and people have always been exceedingly kind to me. They have given to me comforts which they deny themselves. They have provided their tables with delicacies for me which they did not ordinarily enjoy themselves. And in these many homes, I have oftentimes found the afflicted, aged ones, sick ones, defective ones, and many a time I have wished that I had power to heal, that I might make some small return to these dear Christian people for their many kindnesses to me, and some years ago I began to pray on this subject.

I said, "Lord, You have made me a teacher. I have not had the gifts of healing. But people are kind to me wherever I go, and oftentimes they are needy. Many times they are suffering. If You are willing to help me to help them, I should be grateful."

Not a great while after, I was asked to pray in a home where a little child lay already apparently dead. The nurse had been told that it was unnecessary to return, that there was nothing to be done. Two physicians told me that there was nothing to be done. To me the child looked practically dead already. There was no color; there was no apparent breath. The little fellow seemed all ready to be buried. That was at 11 o'clock in the morning. At 5 o'clock in the afternoon the pink had come back into his cheeks and he was sleeping peacefully, quietly, breathing as well as you do—perhaps better. He went through my yard the other day—a stout little lad of five or six years. I said to my wife, "Is not that the baby for whom we prayed?" She said, "Yes, it is he." If only I had known how to pray earlier, if only I had lived more humbly, I am sure it would have kept death out of my own house. Since I learned to pray, I am sure that God has done this for me.

It seems to me the most stupid thing for men to profess to doubt the power of God or the disposition of God to heal the sick or even, if He pleases, to raise the dead. I have seen a dry and burning earth on which for weeks no rain had fallen, softened and freshened, cleared and vivified by refreshing showers that followed prayer for rain, prayer in church, prayer in our home circle, prayer in my own room. People who profess to know occasionally tell me that there is no connection between these prayers and the results which followed. I am not careful to answer them. I am a witness to the facts. I know them to be true. I believe the story of Elijah as easily as I believe that the sun will rise tomorrow. It is not an effort for my faith. It seems to me perfectly natural that God should in a time like Elijah's put the power to open and close the skies into a human hand.

I believe today that if ministers were like him in their humility, in their obedience, in their self-denial, it would be perfectly possible for God to trust them with the key to the skies. I have not the slightest doubt of it and that He would do so. But a fleshly, ease-loving, man-honoring, time-serving church will have very little power about the skies. It will have very little faith because it has very little power. I have seen even demons go out of my children. I have known them to go out of my own heart. I have seen them go out of the hearts of other people in answer to prayer. Why should it be thought incredible with men that God should change the order of nature? If He created it, and if there is good and sufficient reason for alteration, why should He not pull the reversing lever? If men can steer a big motor car forward, backward, or around an obstacle, why should not God propel a world or a nation or an individual in like manner?

I would that burdened ones who have never learned that God can and does interfere in human affairs for the good of His people might believe this. I do not think that there is any one thing which burdened, sick, perplexed, harassed, tempted, tempest-tossed, despondent, despairing people need like this faith of God and it is free for the asking. "Whosoever will, let him take the water of life freely" (Rev. 22:17).

It is in this element [of unction] that the pulpit oftener fails than in any other element. Just at this all-important point it lapses. Learning it may have, brilliancy and eloquence may delight and charm, sensation or less offensive methods may bring the populace in crowds, mental power may impress and enforce truth with all its resources; but without this unction, each and all these will be but as the fretful assault of the waters on a Gibraltar. Spray and foam may cover and spangle; but the rocks are there still, unimpressed and un-impressible. The human heart can no more be swept of its hardness and sin by these human forces than these rocks can be swept away by the ocean's ceaseless flow.

This unction is the consecration force, and its presence the continuous test of that consecration. It is this divine anointing on the preacher that secures his consecration to God and His work. Other forces and motives may call him to the work, but this only is consecration. A separation to God's work by the power of the Holy Spirit is the only consecration recognized by God as legitimate.

The unction, the divine unction, this heavenly anointing, is what the pulpit needs and must have. This divine and heavenly oil put on it by the imposition of God's hand must soften and lubricate the whole man—heart, head, spirit—until it separates him with a mighty separation from all earthly, secular, worldly, selfish motives and aims, separating him to everything that is pure and Godlike.

E.M. Bounds

162

CHAPTER TWENTY-TWO

GOD CHANGES SINFUL HEARTS

I have referred several times in this writing to the fact that God in answer to prayer changes the hearts of men. I desire, since the matter is of such importance, to deal with it, if not more explicitly, at least at somewhat greater length, for our lives are determined very largely by the lives of those about us; and in turn, our lives affect them; and if in either case the influence is unhappy, there is call for change. I suppose that the average man would say that it would be easier for God to change a man's mind than to send water out of a rock or bread from the clouds. I look upon this impression as absolutely mistaken. In my judgment, it is far easier to change the order of *things* than to change the movements of a human soul.

I believe that a real conversion is a far greater marvel than a resurrection from the dead. It is my conviction that men who doubt God's power to interfere with nature doubt His power to interfere with human souls. I think that most of them in their heart of hearts disbelieve in the regeneration of a human soul. They all believe in the duty of improvement and the possibility of improvement; but so far as I am acquainted with them, they doubt miraculous changes in human souls. I do not know what they make of such Bible records as that concerning Saul of Tarsus. I do not see how they can believe that. If they did, they would find it easy to believe that God, in case of need, could do such work nowadays and that if there were a reason for it, He would do it. But leaving this question to those concerned, I wish to record my faith that God oftentimes answers our prayers by changing the sinful hearts of men. That is, He grants us the thing that we desire by bringing an influence to bear on the hearts of individuals, so that they cease to hinder and become helpers toward the thing which we rightfully ask from God, which we ask in the name of Jesus, which we ask praying in the Spirit, which we ask having the mind of Christ.

Abusive People

I read many years ago of a wife who had become a Christian. Her husband was one of the coarse, loudmouthed, ill-mannered, indecent heathen that we occasionally find in Christian lands. He objected to her going to the meetings. He threatened that if she did not discontinue her interest in her soul's welfare, that he would turn her out of the house. She had had abundant occasion in a heartbroken married life to know that he was capable of doing all that he threatened; but deprived of most of the comforts of this life, she had made up her mind that she would not fail of the life eternal and so, with many prayers, she went steadfastly on.

At last the time came when members were to be received into the church. She had already confessed her faith as a Christian and had asked for admission into the church. Her demonized husband said to her during the week preceding the Sabbath on which members were to be received, "Do you intend to join the church?"

"Yes, Husband, I do."

"Well, you understand that when you join that church you go out of this house."

"Yes, I understand," and still she waited in heart before God, and kept waiting. At last the day came—Sabbath morning. They lived some miles from the village. She had been walking to and from the meetings, though there were plenty of horses and conveyances on the premises.

This Sabbath morning early, he again questioned her as to her purpose and she again declared her intention of going forward to unite with the church. Once more he threatened her with banishment from home should she do so, and still once again she declared her intention of obeying God rather than man. He was ill at ease—demonized persons are always ill at ease. If one possessed by the demon of pride, or vanity, or lust, or lying, or dishonesty, or any other demon, reads these words, he shall be my witness. He was ill at ease. The sky rebuked him. The earth rebuked him. His own heart rebuked him. God rebuked him and at last, surrendering to God, he came into the house and said to his wife, "I will have the team ready shortly." The evil spirit went out and Christ came in.

Warlords

How are we to explain the fact that rulers who call themselves Christians can grind the faces of millions of peasants to build guns and warships and rifles and prepare ammunition and train millions of men to kill one another with no cause, by thousands and tens of thousands and hundreds of thousands, to widow wives, to orphan children, to destroy all the foundations of moral excellencies among the people? How are we to explain the fact that these miserable enemies of the human race can do such things as they are doing before our eyes today? There is only one explanation. They are demonized. And why are not these demons cast out? Largely because the preachers to whom these men have listened do not believe in the miracle-working power of God at all.

These preachers have been teaching that it is impossible for God to work miracles, that it is impossible that Jesus should have been born as the Bible says He was. That it is impossible that He should have wrought the works which the Bible assigns to Him. That it is impossible that His death should have a redemptive character so that He was wounded for our transgressions, bruised for our iniquities, and that by His stripes we should be healed. They have been teaching that it is impossible that He should have risen from the dead, that He should have ascended quietly from the Mount of Olives until clouds received Him out of their sight. All these things are declared to be impossible by the preachers who have been instructing these warlords.

And what is the natural result? Precisely what you see before you—men who believe in no God, men who believe in the righteousness of wholesale murder and slaughter, who can see the bodies of dear young soldiers, the kisses of their mothers yet warm upon their lips, reduced to ashes or ground up in the mire by the wheels of the guns. We shall have more of these wars, of course we shall have more, until men repent and turn to God and unless some way or other they come to believe that the God who made the world can rule it, that the God who made man can change the heart of man.

Greedy People

I knew of a man whose moral life was exemplary in every respect but one—he was greedy. He was a member of the church, but he loved money. He paid money to support the church because he ruled it, because it enabled him to show his power over his brethren, and still he gathered up and put away more money. His minister went to see him on a sick bed and was faithful to him. He said to him, "Brother, you are sick because you are selfish. If you do not get victory over your greed and avarice, you will probably die. I fear that your very soul is in peril. Certainly your life is being lost." The minister went away. The sick miser was angry; at the same time, he was unable to get away from the truth.

There came to his house not a great while thereafter a poor missionary from China, heartbroken with the miseries of the uncounted millions, willing to risk his own life, to sacrifice his comfort, to live an exile from his home and friends, if only he could see salvation for the poor Chinese. He knew the reputation of this miserly church member. He knew that there was no human reason to suppose that he could receive a penny from him. On the other hand, he knew that he would be welcomed in the rich man's house, for it was a part of his office as lord of the church to take care of guests. He was glad to have missionaries in his splendid house. They cost him practically nothing, and they ministered to his vanity and self-conceit. This poor missionary, having traveled all up and down the Atlantic coast, barely receiving his traveling expenses, had given up hope and said nothing to this stingy church member about his work.

Ordinarily the man did not care to hear about such work. He liked to talk about himself and what he had done and what he was proposing to do. But on this occasion he was strangely moved to inquire about the work in China. The missionary, of course, was glad to tell him about the experiences of months. The weight of the burden on his heart had so benumbed him that he did not even then have any expectation of relief from this source. He knew he was welcome to stay, that he would have a good room in which to sleep and plenty of good food to eat, and that was all that he expected this man to do for him or for the work.

The evening wore on, and finally the rich man drew out a checkbook, filled in a check and signed it. Blotting it and folding it and handing it to the missionary, he said, "This will help you some in your work." Ten dollars for such a cause would have been a large gift from that avaricious man. The missionary was surprised to receive anything. He sorely needed $25,000 to put up buildings so that the workers might be housed and the work might go forward. When he reached his room, almost paralyzed with his burden, he opened the check. It was for $25,000, good in any bank in the world! It lifted his load and sent him on his way to China with a thankful heart.

God Can Move the Human Heart

People who do not know that God can change the hearts of other folk are greatly to be pitied. People who know that God can do this, and that He does do this in answer to prayer and thus answers many other prayers, are greatly to blame if they fail to exercise this God-given privilege. Who of us is there who can plead not guilty to the one or the other of these infidelities?

Some of us do not know that God can really change the hearts of man. We think if they are changed we are to change them. Beyond doubt, we do have our work to perform in this direction, but we can never change the hearts of men. We cannot change even our own hearts. We have many of us tried to a thousand times and failed. How then shall we change the hearts of others?

If men's hearts are not changed, then many prayers which we ourselves have offered must remain unanswered, for God operates very largely through men and He operates through men according to their hearts. If their hearts are wrong, the work they do will be wrong. If their hearts are changed and become right, then their works will be changed. Oh that there might be throughout the length and breadth of the church of Jesus Christ today a new and vital faith in the power of God to answer prayers by changing the hearts of men.

How many fathers and mothers would find the task of lifting their children lightened! How many pastors would find all the schemes of the church vivified, quickened into new life because the hearts of officers and people had been vivified and quickened into new life! How many teachers would find their task lightened, if they could only believe that God can change the hearts of men and thus answer their prayers!

Of what use is it to scold, to fret, to whine, when we have access to the throne of God and when God can change the lives of men, and changing the lives of men, provide means, remove difficulties, energize in every way the good things which His honest people desire to see done!

Scripture quotations in this book are from the
King James Version of the Bible.

Recommended Dewey Decimal Classification: 264.1
Suggested Subject Heading: PRAYER

Library of Congress Catalog Card Number: 84-52033
ISBN: 0-89693-520-5

VICTOR BOOKS
A division of SP Publications, Inc.
Wheaton, Illinois 60187

GETTING THINGS FROM GOD

CHARLES A. BLANCHARD

While this book is designed for
your personal enjoyment,
it is also intended for group study.
A Leader's Guide with Victor
Multiuse Transparency Masters
is available from your local bookstore
or from the publisher.

VICTOR

BOOKS a division of SP Publications, Inc.
WHEATON. ILLINOIS 60187

Offices also in
Whitby, Ontario, Canada
Amersham-on-the-Hill, Bucks, England